Ergebnisse der Mathematik und ihrer Grenzgebiete

Band 52

Herbert S. Wilf

Finite Sections of Some Classical Inequalities

Springer-Verlag Berlin · Heidelberg · New York 1970

Herbert S. Wilf

University of Pennsylvania, Philadelphia, Pa.

Printed in Germany. Title No. 4596

Printed by Brühlsche Universitätsdruckerei, Gießen

Preface

Hardy, Littlewood and Pólya's famous monograph on inequalities [17] has served as an introduction to hard analysis for many mathematicians. Some of its most interesting results center around Hilbert's inequality and generalizations. This family of inequalities determines the best bound of a family of operators on l^p. When such inequalities are restricted only to finitely many variables, we can then ask for the rate at which the bounds of the restrictions approach the uniform bound.

In the context of Toeplitz forms, such research was initiated over fifty years ago by Szegö [37], and the chain of ideas continues to grow strongly today, with fundamental contributions having been made by Kac, Widom, de Bruijn, and many others.

In this monograph I attempt to draw together these lines of research from the point of view of sharpenings of the classical inequalities of [17]. This viewpoint leads to the exclusion of some material which might belong to a broader-based discussion, such as the elegant work of Baxter, Hirschman and others on the strong Szegö limit theorem, and the inclusion of other work, such as that of de Bruijn and his students, which is basically nonlinear, and is therefore in some sense disjoint from the earlier investigations.

I am grateful to Professor Halmos for inviting me to prepare this volume, and to Professors John and Olga Todd for several helpful comments.

Philadelphia, Pa. H. S. W.
Spring, 1970

Contents

CHAPTER I

Basic Results

1.1 Introduction

We consider any classical inequality of the form

$$f(x_1, x_2, \ldots) < A g(x_1, x_2, \ldots) \tag{1.1}$$

where the x_i are real variables and where A is a best possible constant; that is, if A were replaced by any smaller number there would exist a set of x for which (1.1) would be false.

If we restrict (1.1) to just n variables, we find that

$$f(x_1, x_2, \ldots, x_n, 0, 0, \ldots) < A g(x_1, x_2, \ldots, x_n, 0, 0, \ldots) \tag{1.2}$$

which is surely true, but in general will no longer be best possible for each n. Indeed, we should expect to find a sequence of constants A_n $(n = 1, 2, \ldots)$ such that

$$f(x_1, x_2, \ldots, x_n, 0, 0, \ldots) \leqq A_n g(x_1, x_2, \ldots, x_n, 0, 0, \ldots) \tag{1.3}$$

and

$$A - A_n \to 0 \qquad (n \to \infty) . \tag{1.4}$$

The object of this volume may now be concisely stated: to investigate refinements of the assertion (1.4) and to elucidate some of the theory which enters into such investigations. This theory includes, at one point or another, functional analysis, orthogonal polynomials, potential theory, Dirichlet series, number theory and other branches of analysis. It forms a coherent and deep theoretical structure, still in a stage of vigorous development, which makes use of and itself illuminates substantial bodies of related mathematics. Numerous areas remain unclear, as we shall try to point out along the way, and these insure the continuing development of the subject in the future.

In this first chapter we summarize some of the classical results on which the field is based. These include the inequalities of Hilbert, Hardy, and Carleman, as well as the basic properties of Toeplitz forms.

In Chapter 2 we give the theory of Toeplitz integral kernels, due to Widom. This will then be related to another class of integral kernels and, through them, back to the classical inequalities. Applications to Dirichlet series will be given.

Chapter 3 is concerned with Hankel forms and their spectral theory. There we discuss the boundedness of such forms, their lowest eigenvalues, and connections with orthogonal polynomials on a curve in the complex plane. We obtain the behavior of the lowest eigenvalue of sections of a matrix of moments, which yields the asymptotic condition number of the Hilbert matrix as a special case.

Finally, Chapter 4 is devoted to a study of those inequalities which do not assert the boundedness of some linear operator on l^2. Here much of the general theory is inapplicable and new methods have to be introduced to deal with special problems. The truncated version of Carleman's inequality is given, to introduce the ideas, and extensions of the method to more general inequalities in l^p are presented.

1.2 The Hilbert Matrix

As a striking example of our results, as we obtain them, we shall refer often to the Hilbert matrix, which in general form is

$$H_\lambda = (1/(i+j+\lambda)) \qquad (i,j=1,2,3,\ldots). \tag{1.5}$$

It was introduced by Hilbert as an example of a bounded linear operator on l^2 whose row and column sums are divergent. The special position of the matrix H_0 in the present context is that it stands at the confluence of two streams of investigations. First, H_0 is a Hankel matrix, that is, a matrix whose i,j entry depends only on $i+j$. Secondly, $1/(i+j)$ are the values of a function $(x+y)^{-1}$ which is homogeneous of degree -1. We will see that after a simple transformation such functions are Toeplitz kernels. Hence H_0 is at once Hankel and Toeplitz, and so it is involved simultaneously with the developments of both Chapters 2 and 3.

We give the elementary theory of H_λ here. First, to evaluate the determinant $D_n(\lambda)$ of the first n rows and columns of H_λ we use Cauchy's formula

$$\det\left(\frac{1}{a_r+b_s}\right)_{r,s=1}^{n} = \frac{\prod\limits_{j<i}(b_i-b_j)(a_i-a_j)}{\prod\limits_{i,j=1}^{n}(a_i+b_j)}. \tag{1.6}$$

A proof can be found in Pólya-Szegö [32]. Putting $a_r=b_r=r+\lambda/2$, $r=1,2,\ldots,n$, one finds

$$D_n(\lambda)=\det\left(\frac{1}{i+j+\lambda}\right)_{i,j=1}^{n}=\left[\prod_{j=1}^{n-1} j!\right]^2 \prod_{j=2}^{n+1}\frac{\Gamma(j+\lambda)}{\Gamma(n+j+\lambda)}. \tag{1.7}$$

This determinant is extremely small. In fact by taking logarithms and using Stirling's formula it is easy to deduce that, for example,

$$D_n(0) \sim K n^{-3/4} 4^{-n^2} (e/2n)^{2n} \quad (n \to \infty). \tag{1.8}$$

It follows that the matrix $H_\lambda]_{i,j=1}^n$ is very nearly singular ("ill-conditioned"), a fact which accounts for its popularity among numerical analysts since it seves as an excellent test for proposed new numerical methods. Since, from (1.7), H_λ is positive definite, one should expect the lowest eigenvalue of its nth section to approach zero very rapidly. We shall make this statement precise in Chapter 3.

Hilbert's inequality states that H_0 is a bounded operator in l^2. More precisely it asserts that if $\{x_j\}_{j=1}^\infty$ is l^2 and not $\equiv 0$, then

$$\sum_{m,n=1}^{\infty} \frac{x_m x_n}{m+n} < \pi \sum_{m=1}^{\infty} x_m^2 \tag{1.9}$$

and the constant π cannot be replaced by a smaller one. The integral analogue holds that if f, g are $\mathscr{L}_2$ then

$$\int_0^\infty \int_0^\infty \frac{f(x) f(y)}{x+y}\, dx\, dy < \pi \int_0^\infty f^2(x)\, dx \tag{1.10}$$

unless $f(x) \equiv 0$, with π again the best possible constant.

Numerous proofs have been published. We give here the one which generalizes most readily to the theorems about finite sections which are our ultimate concern. This proof, due to Schur [34], actually handles the situation where we have a kernel $K(x, y)$ which is homogeneous of degree -1, *i.e.*,

$$K(\alpha x, \alpha y) = \alpha^{-1} K(x, y)$$

and a matrix K whose entries are $K(m, n)$ $(m, n = 1, 2, \ldots)$. The theorem gives explicitly the bound, corresponding to π in (1.9), for such kernels. It is

Theorem 1.1. *Let $K(x, y)$ be nonnegative, symmetric, homogeneous of degree -1, and let*

$$M = \int_0^\infty K(x, 1) x^{-1/2}\, dx. \tag{1.11}$$

Suppose that $K(x, 1)/\sqrt{x}$ decreases strictly with x and $K(1, y)/\sqrt{y}$ decreases with y. Then

$$\sum_{m,n=1}^{\infty} K(m, n) x_m x_n < M \sum x_m^2 \tag{1.12}$$

unless $x_m \equiv 0$ $(m = 1, 2, \ldots)$. The constant M is best possible.

Proof. We have

$$K(r/n,1)\,(r/n)^{-1/2}\,1/n < \int_{\frac{r-1}{n}}^{r/n} K(x,1)x^{-1/2}dx$$

by the monotonicity hypothesis. Hence, summing from $r=1$ to ∞,

$$\sum_{r=1}^{\infty} K(r/n,1)\,(r/n)^{-1/2}\,1/n < \int_0^{\infty} K(x,1)x^{-1/2}dx = M\,. \tag{1.13}$$

Similarly we obtain

$$\sum_{r=1}^{\infty} K(1,r/m)\,(r/m)^{-1/2}\,1/m < \int_0^{\infty} K(1,y)y^{-1/2}dy = M\,. \tag{1.14}$$

It follows that

$$\begin{aligned}\sum_{m,n=1}^{\infty} K(m,n)x_m x_n &= \sum_{m,n=1}^{\infty}\left\{x_m K(m,n)^{1/2}\left(\frac{m}{n}\right)^{1/4}\right\}\left\{x_n K(m,n)^{1/2}\left(\frac{n}{m}\right)^{1/4}\right\} \\ &\leqq \left\{\sum_{m=1}^{\infty} x_m^2 \sum_{n=1}^{\infty} K(m,n)\left(\frac{m}{n}\right)^{1/2}\right\}^{1/2}\left\{\sum_{n=1}^{\infty} x_n^2 \sum_{m=1}^{\infty} K(m,n)\left(\frac{n}{m}\right)^{1/2}\right\}^{1/2}\end{aligned} \tag{1.15}$$

by Schwarz' inequality. But

$$\begin{aligned}\sum_{m=1}^{\infty} x_m^2 \sum_{n=1}^{\infty} K(m,n)\left(\frac{m}{n}\right)^{1/2} &= \sum_{m=1}^{\infty} x_m^2 \sum_{n=1}^{\infty} K\left(1,\frac{n}{m}\right)\left(\frac{n}{m}\right)^{-1/2} 1/m \\ &< \sum_{m=1} x_m^2 M\end{aligned}$$

where (1.14) and the homogeneity of K were used. Treating the second factor on the right side of (1.15) similarly we obtain the result stated. To show that the constant M is best possible, one chooses the sequence

$$x_m = \begin{cases} 1/\sqrt{m} & m \leqq N \\ 0 & m > N \end{cases}$$

and lets $N \to \infty$. We do not give this calculation here as it will follow from our later work that M of (1.11) is the best uniform constant (see Section 2.5).

For the corresponding integral problem we have

$$\int_0^{\infty}\int_0^{\infty} K(x,y)f(x)f(y)\,dx\,dy < M\int_0^{\infty} f(x)^2 dx \tag{1.16}$$

where M is again given by (1.11), the proof, due to Schur [3] is even easier. We have

$$\int_0^\infty \int_0^\infty K(x,y)f(x)f(y)\,dx\,dy = \int_0^\infty f(x)\,dx \int_0^\infty xK(x,xu)f(xu)f(xu)\,du$$

$$= \int_0^\infty f(x)\,dx \int_0^\infty K(1,u)f(xu)\,du$$

$$= \int_0^\infty K(1,u)\,du \int_0^\infty f(x)f(xu)\,dx$$

$$< \int_0^\infty K(1,u)\,du \left\{\int_0^\infty f(x)^2\,dx\right\}^{1/2} \left\{\int_0^\infty f(xu)^2\,dx\right\}^{1/2}$$

$$= \left\{\int_0^\infty K(1,u)u^{-1/2}\,du\right\} \int_0^\infty f(x)^2\,dx$$

$$= M \int_0^\infty f(x)^2\,dx$$

as required.

With reference to the Hilbert matrix H_0, or more generally, with reference to a kernel satisfying the conditions of the theorem, we can now formulate some of our problems very precisely. Let K_n denote the nth section of K, *i.e.*, the matrix formed from the first n rows and columns of the array $K(r,s)$. Consider the best possible constant for the inequality

$$\sum_{\mu,\nu=1}^{n} K(\mu,\nu)x_\mu x_\nu \leqq \lambda_n \sum_{\mu=1}^{n} x_\mu^2 .$$

By well known extremal properties of eigenvalues of symmetric matrices, λ_n is the largest eigenvalue of K_n. By Theorem 1.1, $\lambda_n < M$, and $\lambda_n \to M$ as $n \to \infty$.

Let $\lambda_1^{(n)} \leqq \lambda_2^{(n)} \leqq \cdots \leqq \lambda_n^{(n)}$ denote all of the eigenvalues of K_n.

Problem 1: What can be said about the asymptotic behavior of $M - \lambda_n^{(n)}$ as $n \to \infty$?

Problem 2: What can be said about the distribution of the $\lambda_j^{(m)}$ in the interval $(0, M)$, as $n \to \infty$?

Problem 3: For the Hilbert matrix, what can be said about the rate at which $\lambda_1^{(n)} \to 0$?

In all three cases we shall provide quite satisfactory answers, not only for the Hilbert matrix, but for large families of operators which include it.

1.3 Nonlinear Operators

Similar questions arise for inequalities in infinitely many variables even if the inequality is not about bounds for operators on a Hilbert space. As an example, consider

Theorem 1.2 (Carleman's inequality). *Let* $x_1, x_2, \ldots$ *be nonnegative and not all zero. Then*

$$\sum_{n=1}^{\infty} (x_1 x_2 x_3 \ldots x_n)^{1/n} < e \sum_{n=1}^{\infty} x_n . \tag{1.17}$$

The constant e is the best possible.

Proof (Carleman [6], Pólya [31]). By the arithmetic-geometric mean inequality applied to $\{m x_m\}$ we obtain

$$\begin{aligned}\sum_{m=1}^{\infty} (x_1 x_2 \ldots x_m)^{1/m} &= \sum_{m=1}^{\infty} \{(x_1)(2x_2)(3x_3)\cdots(m x_m)/m!\}^{1/m} \\ &\leqq \sum_{m=1}^{\infty} m!^{-1/m}(1/m) \sum_{j=1}^{m} j x_j \\ &< \sum_{m=1}^{\infty} (e/(m+1)m) \sum_{j=1}^{m} j x_j \\ &= e \sum_{j=1}^{\infty} j x_j \sum_{m=j}^{\infty} 1/m(m+1) \\ &= e \sum_{j=1}^{\infty} x_j\end{aligned}$$

where we have used the relation $m!^{1/m} > (m+1)/e$. If we choose

$$x_m = \begin{cases} 1/m & m \leqq N \\ 0 & m > N \end{cases}$$

then

$$\begin{aligned}\left(\sum_{n=1}^{\infty} (x_1 \ldots x_n)^{1/n}\right) \Big/ \left(\sum_{n=1}^{\infty} x_n\right) &\sim \left(\sum_{n=1}^{N} 1/(n!)^{1/n}\right) \Big/ (\log N) \\ &\sim e \qquad (N \to \infty)\end{aligned}$$

so the constant e is best possible.

Now, if λ_n is the best constant for the inequality

$$\sum_{m=1}^{n} (x_1 x_2 \ldots x_m)^{1/m} \leqq \lambda_n \sum_{m=1}^{n} x_m \tag{1.18}$$

we have $\lambda_n < e$ and $e - \lambda_n \to 0$ as $n \to \infty$. We may ask for the asymptotic behavior of $e - \lambda_n$ for $n \to \infty$, and we shall answer this question in Chapter 4.

This problem is apparently a completely different sort of question from the l^2 questions regarding linear operators. There is however a connecting link which has, at this writting, been only partly exploited. This link is the theory of inequalities in l^p. Indeed, suppose we accept, for a moment, the truth of Hardy's inequality

$$\sum_{n=1}^{\infty} \left(\frac{x_1 + \cdots + x_n}{n} \right)^p < 1/(1-1/p)^p \sum_{n=1}^{\infty} x_n^p \tag{1.19}$$

where $p > 0$, and the x_i are nonnegative and not all zero. Then writing $x_m = y_m^{1/p}$ $(m = 1, 2, \ldots)$

$$\sum_{n=1}^{\infty} \left(\frac{y_1^{1/p} + \cdots + y_{nn}^{1/p}}{n} \right)^p < 1/(1-1/p)^p \sum_{n=1}^{\infty} y_n$$

and letting $p \to \infty$ we obtain Carleman's inequality, aside from the replacement of a "$<$" by a "$\leqq$". But Theorem 1.1 has an immediate generalization to inequalities in l^p involving homogeneous kernels of degree -1. This generalization is due to Hardy, Littlewood, and Pólya [17] and is

Theorem 1.3. *Under the hypotheses of Theorem 1.1 write*

$$k = \int_0^{\infty} K(x, 1) x^{-1/p} dx \tag{1.20}$$

where $p > 1$, *and let* $1/p + 1/p' = 1$. *Then*

$$\sum_{m,n=1}^{\infty} K(m, n) x_m y_n < k \left(\sum x_m^p\right)^{1/p} \left(\sum y_n^{p'}\right)^{1/p'} \tag{1.21}$$

and

$$\sum_{n=1}^{\infty} \left(\sum_{m=1}^{\infty} K(m, n) x_m \right)^p < k^p \sum x_m^p \tag{1.22}$$

unless $x_m \equiv 0$.

The proof is a direct generalization of that of Theorem 1.1, and is omitted. With

$$K(x, y) = \begin{cases} 1/y & (x \leqq y) \\ 0 & (x > y) \end{cases} \tag{1.23}$$

we satisfy the hypotheses of Theorem 1.3 and obtain Hardy's inequality from (1.22). At present, no general theory is known which gives the rate of approach of the best possible constant λ_n in the inequality

$$\sum_{r=1}^{n}\left(\sum_{s=1}^{n} K(s,r)x_s\right)^p \leqq \lambda_n^p \sum_{r=1}^{n} x_r^p \tag{1.24}$$

to its limit k, of (1.20). We regard this as one of the major unsolved problems of the subject. We shall make some observations on this question in Chapter 4, but in contrast to the very general treatment of Chapters 2 and 3, Chapter 4 will deal specifically with Hardy's and Carleman's inequalities.

1.4 Toeplitz Forms

In this section we summarize basic facts about Toeplitz forms. For a more complete treatment the reader should consult the work of Grenander and Szegö [16], or the paper of Kac, Murdock, and Szegö [26]. If f is real, periodic, and $\mathscr{L}(-\pi,\pi)$, let

$$a_n = (1/2\pi)\int_0^{2\pi} f(t)e^{-int}dt \qquad (n = \ldots, -1, 0, 1, \ldots). \tag{1.25}$$

The nth Toeplitz form associated with f is the quadratic form

$$(x, A_n x) = \sum_{\mu,\nu=0}^{n} a_{\mu-\nu} x_\mu \bar{x}_\nu \qquad (n = 0, 1, 2, \ldots) \tag{1.26}$$

and the Toeplitz matrix associated with f is the matrix

$$A = (a_{\mu-\nu})_{\mu,\nu=0}^{\infty} \tag{1.27}$$

whose sections are $A_n (n = 0, 1, \ldots)$.

Now A_n is an $(n+1)\times(n+1)$ Hermitian matrix, and so it has $n+1$ real eigenvalues, say

$$\lambda_1^{(n)} \leqq \lambda_2^{(n)} \leqq \cdots \leqq \lambda_{n+1}^{(n)}. \tag{1.28}$$

The central question in the theory of Toeplitz forms is the relationship between the distribution of the spectrum (1.28) of A_n and the original function f. First we can substitute (1.25) into (1.26) and find

$$(x, A_n x) = \frac{1}{2\pi}\int_0^{2\nu} |x_0 + x_1 \bar{e}^{i\theta} + \cdots + x_n \bar{e}^{in\theta}|^2 f(\theta)d\theta. \tag{1.29}$$

From this representation of Toeplitz forms we can read off several facts.

1°. Suppose $f(\theta) \geqq 0$ *a.e.* Then A_n is positive definite.

2°. Suppose $\operatorname*{ess\,sup}_{0\leqq\theta\leqq 2\pi} f(\theta) = M$. Then

$$(x, A_n x) \leqq M(x, x)$$

and so

$$\lambda_i^{(n)} \leqq M \qquad (i=1, \ldots, n+1; \qquad n=0, 1, \ldots) \tag{1.30}$$

3°. Suppose $\operatorname*{ess\,inf}_{0 \leqq \theta \leqq 2\pi} f(\theta) = m$. Then

$$(x, A_n x) \geqq m(x, x)$$

and so

$$\lambda_i^{(n)} \geqq m \qquad (i=1, \ldots, n+1; \qquad n=0, 1, \ldots). \tag{1.31}$$

Hence if our function f is essentially bounded from above and from below then for the spectrum (1.28) we have

$$m \leqq \lambda_1^{(n)} \leqq \lambda_2^{(n)} \leqq \cdots \leqq \lambda_{n+1}^{(n)} \leqq M, \tag{1.32}$$

in other words all eigenvalues of A_n are in $[m, M]$, for each $n=0, 1, 2, \ldots$.

For more precise information, we may inquire into the details of the distribution of the $\lambda_i^{(n)}$ in $[m, M]$. Here are some of the questions which occur in that regard.

(a) What is the density of eigenvalues in a subinterval of $[m, M]$? Say, if $m < \xi < M$ and $f_n(\xi)$ denotes the fraction of the eigenvalues of A_n which are $\leqq \xi$, what is the behavior of f_n for large n?

(b) When n is large, do the extreme eigenvalues $\lambda_1^{(n)}, \lambda_{n+1}^{(n)}$ approach the endpoints m, M? How fast?

(c) What is the behavior of $\lambda_k^{(n)}$ for fixed $k, n \to \infty$?

Theorem 1.3. *For $n \to \infty$ we have*

$$\frac{1}{n+1}\{\#\ \textit{of}\ \lambda_i^{(n)}\ \textit{which are} \leqq \xi\} \to \frac{1}{2\pi} \times \textit{measure of}\ \{x \mid f(x) \leqq \xi\}. \tag{1.33}$$

This theorem is due to Szegö [37]. It shows that asymptotically the distribution of the eigenvalues mimics the distribution of values of the function f. Yet more than this is true, for Szegö actually showed that if $F(\lambda)$ is any Riemann-integrable function on $[m, M]$, $-\infty < m < M < \infty$, then

$$\lim_{n \to \infty} \frac{F(\lambda_1^{(n)}) + \cdots + F(\lambda_{n+1}^{(n)})}{n+1} = \frac{1}{2\pi} \int_{-\pi}^{\pi} F[f(t)]\,dt. \tag{1.34}$$

Evidently Theorem 1.3 is the special case

$$F(\lambda) = \begin{cases} 1 & m \leqq \lambda \leqq \xi \\ 0 & \text{otherwise} \end{cases}$$

of (1.34). The special case $F(\lambda)=\log\lambda$ yields the asymptotic behavior of Toeplitz determinants in the form

$$\lim_{n\to\infty} \det A_n^{1/n+1} = \exp \frac{1}{2\pi} \int_{-\pi}^{\pi} \log f(t)dt \tag{1.35}$$

provided $m>0$.

The above results, whose proofs nay be found in the references cited, constitute a rather complete answer to question (a). Further, they supply an affirmative answer to the first part of question (b). The second part of question (b) and question (c) were answered for the first time by Kac, Murdock, and Szegö [26]. In the next chapter we derive a somewhat stronger result, due to Widom, and so we postpone a discussion of this point.

There are integral analogues of all of these questions. In place of (1.25) we have

$$\varrho(\xi) = \frac{1}{2\pi} \int_0^{2\pi} f(t) e^{-i\xi t} dt$$

and the quadratic form

$$(x, \varrho_A x) = \int_{-A}^{A} \int_{-A}^{A} \varrho(u-v) x(u) \overline{x(v)} du dv .$$

Corresponding to (1.28), the eigenvalues of ϱ_A are defined by

$$\lambda \phi(x) = \int_{-A}^{A} \varrho(x-y) \phi(y) dy$$

where the "sections" correspond to values of $A\to\infty$. If

$$\lambda_{1,A} \geqq \lambda_{2,A} \geqq \cdots$$

are these eigenvalues we can ask about the rate at which

$$\lambda_{\nu,A} \to M = \max f(t),$$

as $A\to\infty$. Corresponding to the representation (1.29) of the quadratic form, we have

$$(x, \varrho_A x) = \frac{1}{2\pi} \int_0^{2\pi} \left| \int_{-A}^{A} x(u) e^{-iut} \right|^2 f(t) dt \tag{1.36}$$

from which one infers that spectral properties of ϱ_A are bound up with the behavior of f in the neighborhood of its maximum at the origin.

CHAPTER II

Sections of Toeplitz and Hilbert Forms

2.1 Integral Operators

In this chapter we will discuss the spectral theory of Toeplitz integral operators and matrices, and applications of this theory to sections of the classical inequalities. We begin with integral equations of Toeplitz type, *i.e.*,

$$\lambda\phi(x) = \int_{-A}^{A} \varrho(x-y)\phi(y)dy\,. \tag{2.1}$$

We suppose that the kernel $\varrho(x)$ is real and even. If the eigenvalues of (2.1) are denoted by

$$\lambda_{1,A} \geqq \lambda_{2,A} \geqq \cdots \tag{2.2}$$

then we are interested in the behavior, as $A \to \infty$, of $\lambda_{k,A}$ for fixed k. Early results on this question were found by Kac, Murdock, and Szegö [26]. The theorems which we discuss here were developed by H. Widom [49], generalized by him in one direction [47], and then by him in another direction [46], leading to a rather complete description of the N-dimensional version of the question raised above.

We begin with an example. Take $\varrho(x) = e^{-|x|}$ and

$$\begin{aligned} \lambda\phi(x) &= \int_{-A}^{A} \varrho(x-y)\phi(y)dy \\ &= \int_{-A}^{A} e^{-|x-y|}\phi(y)dy \\ &= e^{-x}\int_{-A}^{x} e^{y}\phi(y)dy + e^{x}\int_{x}^{A} e^{-y}\phi(y)dy \qquad (-A<x<A)\,. \end{aligned} \tag{2.3}$$

Differentiating twice, we find

$$\lambda\phi''(x) = (\lambda-2)\phi(x) \tag{2.4}$$

together with the boundary conditions

$$\phi'(-A) = \phi(-A); \qquad \phi'(A) = -\phi(A)\,. \tag{2.5}$$

It is then not difficult to check that the eigenvalues are the roots of the equation $k \tan kA = 1$, where $k = [2/\lambda - 1]^{1/2}$, and thence that

$$\lambda_{\nu, A} = 2 - \pi^2 \nu^2 / 2A^2 + O(A^{-3}) \qquad (A \to \infty) \tag{2.6}$$

for each fixed ν. This behavior is typical.

In general, let us suppose that $\varrho(x) \in L_1(-\infty, \infty)$, and put

$$F(\xi) = \int_{-\infty}^{\infty} e^{i\xi x} \varrho(x) dx . \tag{2.7}$$

Suppose further that

$$\begin{aligned} M = F(0) &= \max_{-\infty < \xi < \infty} F(\xi) \\ &= \int_{-\infty}^{\infty} \varrho(x) dx \end{aligned} \tag{2.8}$$

and that for all $\xi \neq 0$, $|F(\xi)| < M$. Finally, make the temporary assumptions that the Fourier transform $F(\xi)$ is a rational function with simple poles only, and that all zeros $\xi \neq 0$ of the function

$$F(\xi) - M$$

in the complex plane are simple. We will obtain the asymptotic behavior of the eigenvalues under these temporary assumptions, and then, by an approximation argument, remove them.

Now since

$$\varrho(x) = (1/2\pi) \int_{-\infty}^{\infty} e^{-i\xi x} F(\xi) d\xi$$

we can rewrite the integral equation (2.1) in the form

$$\lambda \phi(x) = \frac{1}{2\pi} \int_{-\infty}^{\infty} e^{-i\xi x} F(\xi) d\xi \int_{-A}^{A} e^{i\xi y} \phi(y) dy . \tag{2.9}$$

Since F is a rational function, we have

$$F(\xi) = P(\xi)/Q(\xi) ,$$

say, where P, Q are relatively prime polynomials. Then

$$\begin{aligned} \lambda Q(id/dx)\phi(x) &= \frac{1}{2\pi} \int_{-\infty}^{\infty} \{Q(id/dx) e^{-i\xi x}\} F(\xi) d\xi \int_{-A}^{A} e^{i\xi y} \phi(y) dy \\ &= \frac{1}{2\pi} \int_{-\infty}^{\infty} e^{-i\xi x} Q(\xi) F(\xi) d\xi \int_{-A}^{A} e^{i\xi y} \phi(y) dy \\ &= \frac{1}{2\pi} \int_{-\infty}^{\infty} P(\xi) e^{-i\xi x} d\xi \int_{-A}^{A} e^{i\xi y} \phi(y) dy . \end{aligned}$$

On the other hand, by the Fourier inversion theorem

$$\phi(x)=(1/2\pi)\int_{-\infty}^{\infty} e^{-i\xi x}d\xi \int_{-A}^{A} e^{i\xi y}\phi(y)dy\,.$$

Hence

$$P(id/dx)\phi(x)=(1/2\pi)\int_{-\infty}^{\infty} P(\xi)e^{-i\xi x}d\xi \int_{-A}^{A} e^{i\xi y}\phi(y)dy$$

$$=\lambda Q(id/dx)\phi(x)$$

and so our function $\phi(x)$ satisfies the differential equation

$$P(id/dx)\phi(x)=\lambda Q(id/dx)\phi(x)\,. \tag{2.10}$$

This equation reduces to (2.4) when $F(\xi)=2(1+\xi^2)^{-1}$. Since (2.10) has constant coefficients, its solution will depend on the roots of the equation $F(\xi)=\lambda$. Let $\phi(x)$ be a normalized eigenfunction in the sense that

$$\int_{-A}^{A} |\phi(x)|^2 dx = 1/2\pi\,.$$

Then, multiplying (2.9) by $\phi(x)$ and integrating from $-A$ to A,

$$\lambda = \int_{-\infty}^{\infty} F(\xi)|\Phi(\xi)|^2 d\xi \tag{2.11}$$

where

$$\Phi(\xi)=\int_{-A}^{A} e^{i\xi x}\phi(x)dx$$

and Parseval's identity was used.

Now from (2.11) and the relation

$$\int_{-\infty}^{\infty} |\Phi(\xi)|^2 d\xi = 1$$

it follows that $\lambda < M$, and since for each fixed v, $\lambda_{v,A}\to M$, we can restrict attention to the interval $(M-\delta, M)$.

Next, we can choose δ small enough so that for all $\lambda\in(M-\delta, M)$, $F(\xi)-\lambda$ will have simple zeros only. This is because $F'(\xi)$ is rational, and so has only finitely many zeros, which can be excluded from $(M-\delta, M)$ by choice of δ. Since all zeros are simple, the general solution of (2.10) is a linear combination of exponentials, namely

$$\phi(x)=\sum_{j=1}^{2q} c_j e^{i\xi_j x} \tag{2.12}$$

where $2q$ is the degree of $Q(x)$, and the ξ_j run through the zeros of $F(\xi)-\lambda$.

2.2. Proof for the Rational Fourier Transform-Continued

Let us attempt to determine the constants c_j appearing in (2.12). Substituting (2.12) into (2.9), we find

$$\begin{aligned}\lambda \sum_{j=1}^{2q} c_j e^{i\xi_j x} &= \frac{1}{2\pi} \sum_{j=1}^{2q} c_j \int_{-\infty}^{\infty} e^{-i\xi x} F(\xi) d\xi \int_{-A}^{A} e^{(i\xi y + i\xi_j y)} dy \\ &= \frac{1}{2\pi} \sum_{j=1}^{2q} c_j \int_{-\infty}^{\infty} e^{-i\xi x} F(\xi) \{e^{i(\xi+\xi_j)A} - e^{-i(\xi+\xi_j)A}\} \frac{d\xi}{i(\xi+\xi_j)} .\end{aligned} \tag{2.13}$$

In the integral on the right, the only singularities of the integrand are at the poles of $F(\xi)$. We wish to break it up into two integrals, and evaluate each of them by contour integration. This process will introduce a new singularity at $\xi = -\xi_j$ in each integral. Thus, we first indent the contour with a semicircle of radius ε around $\xi = -\xi_j$ on the real axis. We then split the integral into two terms, $I_1(\varepsilon) - I_2(\varepsilon)$

$$\int_{C\varepsilon} e^{-i\xi x} F(\xi) (e^{i(\xi+\xi_j)A} / i(\xi+\xi_j)) d\xi = I_1(\varepsilon) ,$$

$$\int_{C_\varepsilon} e^{-i\xi x} F(\xi) (e^{-i(\xi+\xi_j)A} / i(\xi+\xi_j)) d\xi = I_2(\varepsilon)$$

where C_ε is the contour shown below:

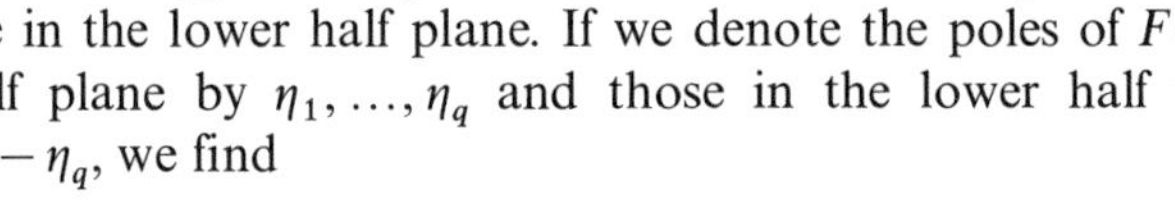

For fixed ε, $I_1(\varepsilon)$ is evaluated by closing C_ε with a large semicircle of radius R in the upper half plane, and letting $R \to \infty$, $I_2(\varepsilon)$ by a similar semicircle in the lower half plane. If we denote the poles of $F(\xi)$ in the upper half plane by $\eta_1, \ldots, \eta_q$ and those in the lower half plane by $-\eta_1, \ldots, -\eta_q$, we find

$$\begin{aligned} I_1(\varepsilon) &= \sum_{k=1}^{q} e^{-i\eta_k x} r_k (e^{i(\xi_j+\eta_k)A} / i(\xi_j + \eta_k)) , \\ I_2(\varepsilon) &= \sum_{k=1}^{q} e^{+i\eta_k x} r_k (e^{-i(\xi_j-\eta_k)A} / i(\xi_j - \eta_k)) + F(\xi_j) e^{i\xi_j x} \end{aligned} \tag{2.14}$$

where r_k is the residue of F at η_k, and we have used the evenness of F. Now $F(\xi_j)=\lambda$, by choice of the ξ_j, hence letting $\varepsilon\to 0$ and substituting in (2.13), we find

$$\begin{aligned}0=&\sum_{k=1}^{q} r_k e^{iA\eta_k}\left(\sum_{j=1}^{2q}(c_j e^{iA\xi_j}/(\xi_j+\eta_k))\right)e^{-i\eta_k x}\\ &+\sum_{k=1}^{q} r_k e^{iA\eta_k}\left(\sum_{j=1}^{2q} c_j e^{-iA\xi_j}/(\xi_j-\eta_k)\right)e^{i\eta_k x}.\end{aligned}\tag{2.15}$$

Equating to zero the coefficients of each $e^{\pm i\eta_k x}$ we find the $2q$ equations in $2q$ unknowns

$$\begin{aligned}&\sum_{j=1}^{2q}(e^{iA\xi_j}/(\xi_j+\eta_k))c_j=0 \qquad (k=1,\dots,q),\\ &\sum_{j=1}^{2q}(e^{-iA\xi_j}/(\xi_j-\eta_k))c_j=0 \qquad (k=1,\dots,q).\end{aligned}\tag{2.16}$$

Now $F(\xi)-M$ has two real zeros, at the origin, and therefore $2q-2$ complex zeros. Of the latter $q-1$ will be in the upper half plane, call them $\xi_2^*,\dots,\xi_q^*$, and the other complex zeros are $-\xi_2^*,\dots,-\xi_q^*$. Hence, if $\lambda\in(M-\delta,M)$, $F(\xi)-\lambda$ has two real zeros, say $\pm\xi_1$, and $2q-2$ complex zeros $\pm\xi_2,\dots,\pm\xi_q$. Then $\xi_j\to\xi_j^*$, as $\lambda\to M$, for each $j=1,\dots,q$. With this new numbering system, the matrix of coefficients of the Eq. (2.16) takes the form

$$A_1=\begin{pmatrix}\dfrac{e^{iA\xi_1}}{\xi_1+\eta_1} & \dfrac{e^{-iA\xi_1}}{-\xi_1+\eta_1} & \cdots & \dfrac{e^{iA\xi_q}}{\xi_q+\eta_1} & \dfrac{e^{-iA\xi_q}}{-\xi_q+\eta_1}\\ \vdots & \vdots & & \vdots & \vdots\\ \dfrac{e^{iA\xi_1}}{\xi_1+\eta_q} & \dfrac{e^{-iA\xi_1}}{-\xi_1+\eta_q} & \cdots & \dfrac{e^{iA\xi_q}}{\xi_q+\eta_q} & \dfrac{e^{-iA\xi_q}}{-\xi_q+\eta_q}\\ \dfrac{e^{-iA\xi_1}}{\xi_1-\eta_1} & \dfrac{e^{iA\xi_1}}{-\xi_1-\eta_1} & \cdots & \dfrac{e^{-iA\xi_q}}{\xi_q-\eta_1} & \dfrac{e^{iA\xi_q}}{-\xi_q-\eta_1}\\ \vdots & \vdots & & \vdots & \vdots\\ \dfrac{e^{-iA\xi_1}}{\xi_1-\eta_q} & \dfrac{e^{iA\xi_1}}{-\xi_1-\eta_q} & \cdots & \dfrac{e^{-iA\xi_q}}{\xi_q-\eta_q} & \dfrac{e^{iA\xi_q}}{-\xi_q-\eta_q}\end{pmatrix}. \tag{2.17}$$

Next, we multiply columns 3 and 4 by $e^{iA\xi_2}$, ..., columns $2q-1$ and $2q$ by $e^{iA\xi_q}$, and if we put

$$D_1=(\det A_1)\exp\left(2iA\sum_{j=1}^{q}\xi_j\right)$$

then

$$D_1=\det\begin{pmatrix}
\dfrac{e^{iA\xi_1}}{\xi_1+\eta_1} & \dfrac{e^{-iA\xi_1}}{-\xi_1+\eta_1} & \dfrac{e^{2iA\xi_2}}{\xi_2+\eta_1} & \dfrac{1}{-\xi_2+\eta_1} & \cdots & \dfrac{1}{-\xi_q+\eta_1}\\
\vdots & \vdots & \vdots & \vdots & & \vdots\\
\dfrac{e^{iA\xi_1}}{\xi_1+\eta_q} & \dfrac{e^{-iA\xi_1}}{-\xi_1+\eta_q} & \dfrac{e^{2iA\xi_2}}{\xi_2+\eta_q} & \dfrac{1}{\xi_2+\eta_q} & \cdots & \dfrac{1}{-\xi_q+\eta_q}\\
\dfrac{e^{-iA\xi_1}}{\xi_1-\eta_1} & \dfrac{e^{iA\xi_1}}{-\xi_1-\eta_1} & \dfrac{1}{\xi_2-\eta_1} & \dfrac{e^{2iA\xi_2}}{-\xi_2-\eta_1} & \cdots & \dfrac{e^{2iA\xi_q}}{-\xi_q-\eta_1}\\
\vdots & \vdots & \vdots & \vdots & & \vdots\\
\dfrac{e^{-iA\xi_1}}{\xi_1-\eta_q} & \dfrac{e^{iA\xi_1}}{-\xi_1-\eta_q} & \dfrac{1}{\xi_2-\eta_q} & \dfrac{e^{2iA\xi_2}}{-\xi_2-\eta_q} & \cdots & \dfrac{e^{2iA\xi_q}}{-\xi_q-\eta_q}
\end{pmatrix}. \tag{2.18}$$

We claim that in the expansion of D_1, any term containing $e^{2iA\xi_j}$ is $O(e^{-2A\mu})$ where μ is a positive constant. Indeed, if

$$\mu=(1/2)\min_{2\leqq j\leqq q}\operatorname{Im}\xi_j^*$$

then for small δ, Im $\xi_j\geqq\mu$, as required. Thus, aside from a term $O(e^{-2A\mu})$ D_1 is

$$\det\begin{pmatrix}
\dfrac{e^{-A\xi_1}}{\xi_1+\eta_1} & \dfrac{e^{-iA\xi_1}}{-\xi_1+\eta_1} & 0 & \dfrac{1}{-\xi_2+\eta_1} & \cdots & 0 & \dfrac{1}{-\xi_q+\eta_1}\\
\vdots & \vdots & \vdots & \vdots & & \vdots & \vdots\\
\dfrac{e^{iA\xi_1}}{\xi_1+\eta_q} & \dfrac{e^{-iA\xi_1}}{-\xi_1+\eta_q} & 0 & \dfrac{1}{-\xi_2+\eta_q} & & 0 & \dfrac{1}{-\xi_q+\eta_q}\\
\dfrac{e^{-iA\xi_1}}{\xi_1-\eta_1} & \dfrac{e^{iA\xi_1}}{-\xi_1-\eta_1} & \dfrac{1}{\xi_2-\eta_1} & 0 & & \dfrac{1}{\xi_q-\eta_1} & 0\\
\vdots & \vdots & \vdots & \vdots & & \vdots & \vdots\\
\dfrac{e^{-iA\xi_1}}{\xi_1-\eta_q} & \dfrac{e^{iA\xi_1}}{-\xi_1-\eta_q} & \dfrac{1}{\xi_2-\eta_q} & 0 & & \dfrac{1}{\xi_q-\eta_q} & 0
\end{pmatrix}.$$

If we expand this determinant we find just two nonvanishing terms,

$$\Delta_1\Delta_4-\Delta_2\Delta_3$$

where

$$\Delta_1 = \det\begin{pmatrix} \dfrac{e^{iA\xi_1}}{\xi_1+\eta_1} & \dfrac{1}{-\xi_2+\eta_1} & \cdots & \dfrac{1}{-\xi_q+\eta_1} \\ \vdots & & & \vdots \\ \dfrac{e^{iA\xi_1}}{\xi_1+\eta_q} & \dfrac{1}{-\xi_2+\eta_q} & \cdots & \dfrac{1}{-\xi_q+\eta_q} \end{pmatrix},$$

$$\Delta_2 = \det\begin{pmatrix} \dfrac{e^{-iA\xi_1}}{-\xi_1+\eta_1} & \dfrac{1}{-\xi_2+\eta_1} & \cdots & \dfrac{1}{-\xi_q+\eta_1} \\ \vdots & \vdots & & \vdots \\ \dfrac{e^{-iA\xi_1}}{-\xi_1+\eta_q} & \dfrac{1}{-\xi_2+\eta_q} & \cdots & \dfrac{1}{-\xi_q+\eta_q} \end{pmatrix},$$

$$\Delta_3 = \det\begin{pmatrix} \dfrac{e^{-iA\xi_1}}{\xi_1-\eta_1} & \dfrac{1}{\xi_2-\eta_1} & \cdots & \dfrac{1}{\xi_q-\eta_1} \\ \vdots & \vdots & & \vdots \\ \dfrac{e^{-iA\xi_1}}{\xi_1-\eta_q} & \dfrac{1}{\xi_2-\eta_q} & \cdots & \dfrac{1}{\xi_q-\eta_q} \end{pmatrix},$$

$$\Delta_4 = \det\begin{pmatrix} \dfrac{e^{iA\xi_1}}{-\xi_1-\eta_1} & \dfrac{1}{\xi_2-\eta_1} & \cdots & \dfrac{1}{\xi_q-\eta_1} \\ \vdots & \vdots & & \vdots \\ \dfrac{e^{iA\xi_1}}{-\xi_1-\eta_q} & \dfrac{1}{\xi_2-\eta_q} & \cdots & \dfrac{1}{\xi_q-\eta_q} \end{pmatrix}.$$

One now observes that Δ_1 and Δ_4 are essentially the same, as are Δ_2, Δ_3. Precisely, we find

$$D_1 = (-1)^q e^{2iA\xi_1} \det\begin{pmatrix} \dfrac{1}{\xi_1+\eta_1} & \dfrac{1}{-\xi_2+\eta_1} & \cdots & \dfrac{1}{-\xi_q+\eta_1} \\ \vdots & \vdots & & \vdots \\ \dfrac{1}{\xi_1+\eta_q} & \dfrac{1}{-\xi_2+\eta_q} & \cdots & \dfrac{1}{-\xi_q+\eta_q} \end{pmatrix}^2 \tag{2.19}$$

$$+ (-1)^{q+1} e^{-2iA\xi_1} \det\begin{pmatrix} \dfrac{1}{\xi_1-\eta_1} & \dfrac{1}{\xi_2-\eta_1} & \cdots & \dfrac{1}{\xi_q-\eta_1} \\ \vdots & \vdots & & \vdots \\ \dfrac{1}{\xi_1-\eta_q} & \dfrac{1}{\xi_2-\eta_q} & \cdots & \dfrac{1}{\xi_q-\eta_q} \end{pmatrix}^2$$

$$+ O(e^{-2A\mu}).$$

These determinants can be evaluated by Cauchy's formula (1.6) with the result that

$$\begin{aligned} D_2 = {} & e^{2iA\xi_1}\Big(\prod_{k\geqq 2}(\xi_1+\xi_k)^2\Big)\Big/\Big(\prod_{k\geqq 1}(\xi_1+\eta_k)^2\Big) \\ & - e^{-2iA\xi_1}\Big(\prod_{k\geqq 2}(\xi_1-\xi_k)^2\Big)\Big/\Big(\prod_{k\geqq 1}(\xi_1-\eta_k)^2\Big) \\ & + O(e^{-2A\mu}) \end{aligned} \tag{2.20}$$

where we have written

$$D_2 = (-1)^q \frac{\prod_{j\geqq 2;\, k\geqq 1}(\xi_j-\eta_k)^2}{\prod_{2\leqq j<k}(\xi_j-\xi_k)^2 \prod_{1\leqq j<k}(\eta_j-\eta_k)^2} D_1 . \tag{2.21}$$

We are interested in the behavior of ξ_1 as $A\to\infty$, where $\xi_1, \ldots, \xi_q$ is a zero of the determinant D_2, and for this purpose we require a crude bound for the eigenvalues λ.

Lemma 1. *There exists a constant $a>0$ such that for all $A>A_0$, we have*

$$\lambda \leqq M - a/A^2 \tag{2.22}$$

where λ is any eigenvalue of our integral equation (2.1).

Proof. If $\sigma^2 = -F''(0) \neq 0$, then for small ξ,

$$F(\xi) \leqq M - \tfrac{1}{4}\sigma^2\xi^2$$

and for $|\xi| \geqq A^{-1}$,

$$\begin{aligned} F(\xi) & \leqq F(1/A) \\ & \leqq M - \sigma^2/4A^2 . \end{aligned}$$

Then from (2.11),

$$\begin{aligned} \lambda & = \int_{-\infty}^{\infty} F(\xi)|\Phi(\xi)|^2 d\xi \\ & = \int_{-1/A}^{1/A} + \int_{|\xi|\geqq 1/A} \\ & \leqq \int_{-1/A}^{1/A}\Big(M-\frac{1}{4}\sigma^2\xi^2\Big)|\Phi(\xi)|^2 d\xi + \Big(M-\frac{\sigma^2}{4A^2}\Big)\int_{|\xi|\geqq 1/A}|\Phi(\xi)|^2 d\xi \\ & = M - \frac{\sigma^2}{4}\Big\{\int_{-1/A}^{1/A}\xi^2|\Phi(\xi)|^2 d\xi + \frac{1}{A^2}\int_{|\xi|\geqq 1/A}|\Phi(\xi)|^2 d\xi\Big\} \\ & = M - \frac{\sigma^2}{4}\Big\{1/A^2 - \int_{-1/A}^{1/A}(1/A^2-\xi^2)|\Phi(\xi)|^2 d\xi\Big\}. \end{aligned} \tag{2.23}$$

Now from

$$\Phi(\xi) = \int_{-A}^{A} e^{i\xi x}\phi(x)dx$$

we find

$$\begin{aligned}|\Phi(\xi)|^2 &\leqq \left\{\int_{-A}^{A} dx\right\}\left\{\int_{-A}^{A} \phi(x)^2 dx\right\}\\ &= 2A \cdot 1/2\pi\\ &= A/\pi\end{aligned}$$

and substituting in (2.23) we have the result stated in the lemma.

Next, if a complex number ξ_1 is specified, then $\lambda = F(\xi_1)$ is determined, and so the other roots of the equation $\lambda = F(\xi)$ are also. Hence we can think of $\pm\xi_2, \ldots, \pm\xi_q$ as functions of ξ_1, and of the determinants $\det A_1$ of (2.17), D_1 of (2.18) and D_2 of (2.21) as functions of a single complex variable ξ_1.

Now when ξ_1 is near 0, λ is near M; indeed, if $|\xi_1| < b/A$, where b is some constant, then, by the lemma,

$$\begin{aligned}M - a/A^2 \geqq \lambda = F(\xi_1)&\\ \geqq M - b'/A^2&\end{aligned}$$

and so if b is small enough and fixed, then for all sufficiently large A the determinant D_2 has no zeros in $|\xi_1| \leqq b/A$. We choose such a b, and choose a large integer N.

Lemma 2. *For $b < \pi/2$, the function $D_2(\xi_1)$ has exactly $2N$ zeros in the annulus*

$$b/A < |\xi_1| < (N + 1/2)\pi/2A \tag{2.24}$$

and these zeros are all simple.

Proof. First, in (2.20), we investigate the error introduced by replacing the ξ_k by ξ_k^*. Since the ξ_k^* are all simple zeros of $F(\xi) - M$, the ξ_k are also simple zeros of $F(\xi) - \lambda$, for δ small enough. Hence all ξ_k are analytic functions of ξ_1 and so is D_2. Differentiating the equation $F(\xi_k) = F(\xi_1)$ with respect to ξ_1,

$$F'(\xi_k)d\xi_k/d\xi_1 = F'(\xi_1) = O(1/A)$$

and therefore

$$d\xi_k/d\xi_1 = O(1/A) \qquad (A \to \infty)$$

for ξ_1 in the annulus (2.24). It follows that

$$\begin{aligned}\xi_k = \xi_k(\xi_1) &= \xi_k(0) + O(\xi_1 d\xi_k/d\xi_1)\\ &= \xi_k^* + O(1/A \cdot 1/A)\\ &= \xi_k^* + O(1/A^2)\,.\end{aligned} \tag{2.25}$$

Define

$$G(\xi) = \Big(\prod_{k\geqq 2}(\xi - \xi_k^*)\Big)\Big/\Big(\prod_{k\geqq 1}(\xi - \eta_k)\Big)\,.$$

Then from (2.20),

$$\begin{aligned}D_2 &= e^{2iA\xi_1}\frac{\prod_{k\geqq 2}(\xi_1 + \xi_k^* + \xi_k - \xi_k^*)^2}{\prod_{k\geqq 1}(\xi_1 + \eta_k)^2} - e^{-2iA\xi_1}\frac{\prod_{k\geqq 2}(\xi_1 - \xi_k^* + \xi_k^* - \xi_k)^2}{\prod_{k\geqq 1}(\xi_1 - \eta_k)^2}\\ &\quad + O(e^{-2A\mu})\\ &= e^{2iA\xi_1}G(-\xi_1)^2 - e^{-2iA\xi_1}G(\xi_1)^2 + O(1/A^2)\\ &= 2iG(0)^2\sin 2A\xi_1 + O(1/A)\,.\end{aligned} \tag{2.26}$$

Suppose ξ_1 is a zero of D_2. Then $\sin 2A\xi_1 = O(1/A)$, and so

$$\xi_1 = \nu\pi/2A + O(1/A) \qquad (\nu = 1, \ldots, N) \tag{2.27}$$

are all of the possible zeros of D_2 in the annulus (2.24). Conversely, D_2 actually does vanish at the points (2.26). To see this, we apply Rouche's theorem to D_2, as given by (2.26), on a circle $C_{\nu,\varepsilon}$, centered at $\nu\pi/2A$, of radius $\varepsilon/2A$. If ξ_1 is on the circumference of $C_{\nu,\varepsilon}$, $\xi_1 = \nu\pi/2A + (\varepsilon/2A)e^{i\psi}$ and so,

$$|2iG(0)^2\sin 2A\xi_1| = 2G(0)^2\,|\sin(\varepsilon e^{i\psi})| > \varepsilon G(0)^2\,.$$

Hence, from (2.26), D_2 and

$$2iG(0)^2\sin 2A\xi_1$$

have the same number of zeros, namely 1, in $C_{\nu,\varepsilon}$, completing the proof of Lemma 2.

From (2.27),

$$\begin{aligned}\lambda = F(\xi_1) &= F(\nu\pi/2A + O(1/A))\\ &= M - (\sigma^2/2)(\nu\pi/2A)^2 + o(1/A^2)\end{aligned}$$

or finally

$$\lambda_{\nu,A} = M - \sigma^2\nu^2\pi^2/8A^2 + o(1/A^2) \qquad (\nu = 1, 2, \ldots,)\,. \tag{2.28}$$

2.3 Statement of the Main Theorem and Proof by Approximation

The result obtained in (2.28) under rather restrictive hypotheses in fact holds quite generally.

Theorem 2.1 (Widom [49]). *Suppose $F(\xi)$, the Fourier transform of $\varrho(x)$, is real, even and satisfies*

$$F(\xi)=O(\xi^{-2}) \qquad (\xi\to\pm\infty).$$

Suppose $M=\max F(\xi)=F(0)$, and that $\xi=0$ is the only ξ at which $F(\xi)=M$. Suppose further that $F''(\xi)$ is continuous near $\xi=0$, and that $\sigma^2=-F''(0)\neq 0$. If $\lambda_{\nu,A}$ is the νth eigenvalue of (2.1), *then for each fixed ν the expansion* (2.28) *holds.*

We have so far proved Theorem 2.1 under the additional hypotheses

(A) $F(\xi)$ is a rational function.

$(\text{B})_1$ All poles of $F(\xi)$ are simple.

$(\text{B})_2$ The zeros of $F(\xi)-M$, aside from $\xi=0$, are simple.

It remains to remove these extra conditions. Now from the Courant-Weyl lemma it follows that if A, B are Hermitian operators on a Hilbert space such that $B-A$ is nonnegative definite then each eigenvalue of A is $\leqq$ the corresponding eigenvalue of B.

The definiteness of an integral operator represented by a kernel $g(x-y)$ on $(-A, A)$ is equivalent to the nonnegativity of its Fourier transform, as is clear from (1.35). Hence if $\varrho(x), \varrho_1(x)$ have transforms $F(\xi), F_1(\xi)$ respectively, and if $F(\xi)\leqq F_1(\xi)$ for all ξ, then, for all A,

$$\lambda_{\nu,A}(F)\leqq\lambda_{\nu,A}(F_1) \qquad (\nu=1,2,\ldots).$$

The conditions (A), $(B)_1$, $(B)_2$ will be removed in reverse order. Thus, suppose first we have $F(\xi)$ satisfying (A), $(B)_1$ but not $(B)_2$. Then for $\varepsilon>0$ put

$$F_\varepsilon(\xi)=F(\xi)+\varepsilon\xi^4/(1+\xi^6). \tag{2.29}$$

Clearly $F_\varepsilon(\xi)$ is a rational function with $F_\varepsilon(0)=M$, $F_\varepsilon''(0)=-\sigma^2$, and for small ε the poles of F_ε are simple.

We have, however

Lemma 3. *The zeros of $F_\varepsilon(\xi)-M$ are simple, aside from $\xi=0$, for all sufficiently small ε.*

Proof. Suppose false. Then for a sequence of $\varepsilon\to 0$ there is a nonzero multiple zero ξ_ε of the equation $F_\varepsilon(\xi_\varepsilon)-M=0$. Since $F(\xi)=O(\xi^{-2})$ at infinity, we have $F_\varepsilon(\xi)-M\to -M$ uniformly in ε. Hence for ξ in $|\xi|\geqq R$, where R is independent of ε, we have $|F_\varepsilon(\xi)-M|\geqq M/2$. Thus all ξ_ε lie in $|\xi|\leqq R$, and there exists a ξ_0 such that $\xi_\varepsilon\to\xi_0$. ξ_0 is evidently a multiple zero of $F(\xi)-M$, of multiplicity $m\geqq 2$.

Now

$$\begin{aligned}F_\varepsilon(\xi_\varepsilon) &= F(\xi_\varepsilon) + \varepsilon(\xi_\varepsilon^4/(1+\xi_\varepsilon^6)) = M \\ &= M + (F^{(m)}(\xi_0)/m!)(\xi_\varepsilon - \xi_0)^m + O(|\xi_\varepsilon - \xi_0|^{m+1}) \\ &\quad + \varepsilon(\xi_\varepsilon^4/1+\xi_\varepsilon^6)\end{aligned}$$

and so

$$(\xi_\varepsilon - \xi_0)^m \sim -(m!\,\xi_0^4/F^{(m)}(\xi_0)(1+\xi_0^6))\cdot\varepsilon \qquad (\varepsilon\to 0)\,. \tag{2.30}$$

But

$$\begin{aligned}0 = F_\varepsilon{}'(\xi_\varepsilon) &= F'(\xi_\varepsilon) + O(|\varepsilon|) \\ &= (F^{(m)}(\xi_0)/(m-1)!)(\xi_\varepsilon - \xi_0)^{m-1} + O(|\varepsilon|)\,.\end{aligned}$$

Thus

$$(\xi_\varepsilon - \xi_0)^{m-1} = O(|\varepsilon|)$$

contradicting (2.30), and proving the lemma.

For small $\varepsilon > 0$ put

$$\varrho_{\pm\varepsilon}(x) = (1/2\pi)\int_{-\infty}^{\infty} e^{-i\xi x}F_{\pm\varepsilon}(\xi)d\xi\,.$$

By (2.28),

$$\lambda_{\nu,A}(F_{\pm\varepsilon}) = M - \sigma^2\pi^2\nu^2/8A^2 + O(1/A^2)$$

and since

$$F_{-\varepsilon}(\xi) \leqq F(\xi) \leqq F_\varepsilon(\xi)$$

we have

$$\lambda_{\nu,A}(F_{-\varepsilon}) \leqq \lambda_{\nu,A}(F) \leqq \lambda_{\nu,A}(F_\varepsilon)$$

which proves the theorem in the case where (A), $(B)_1$ are satisfied but $(B)_2$ is not.

Suppose $F(\xi)$ satisfies (A) but not necessarily $(B)_1$. Then if we define

$$F_\varepsilon(\xi) = P(\xi)/(Q(\xi) + \varepsilon(\xi^4/(1+\xi^6)))$$

we can show, as above, that F_ε satisfies condition (B_1), and proceeding as before, prove the theorem for any rational function.

It remains only to dispose of the condition (A), that F is rational. We need two lemmas on polynomial approximation.

Lemma 4. *Let f be continuous and bounded in* $(0, 1]$. *Then there exists a bounded sequence $\{f_n(x)\}$ of polynomials such that $f_n(x)\to f(x)$ uniformly on every interval $[\delta, 1]$, and $f_n(x) \geqq f(x)$ in* $(0, 1]$.

Proof. If d is a bound for $|f(x)|$ in $(0, 1]$, let

$$g_n(x) = \begin{cases} f(x) & 1/n \leqq x \leqq 1 \\ f(x) + 4d(1 - nx) & 1/2n \leqq x \leqq 1/n \\ f(1/2n) + 2d & 0 \leqq x \leqq 1/2n\,. \end{cases}$$

Then let $f_n(x)$ be any polynomial such that

$$|f_n(x) - (g_n(x) + 1/n)| < 1/2n \qquad (0 \leqq x \leqq 1)\,.$$

Since $g_n(x) = f(x)$ on $[1/n, 1]$, $g_n(x) \geqq f(x)$ in $(0, 1]$, and $g_n(x)$ is continuous on $[0, 1]$, the sequence $f_n(x)$ has the desired properties.

Lemma 5. *If* $f(x) = O(x)$ $(x \to 0)$ *and is continuous on* $[0, 1]$, *there exists a sequence* $\{f_n(x)\}$ *of polynomials satisfying* (a) $f_n(x) \geqq f(x)$, (b) $f_n(0) = 0$, (c) $f_n(x) \to f(x)$ *uniformly on* $[0, 1]$.

Proof. Apply Lemma 4 to $f(x)/x$.

Suppose the function $F(\xi)$ satisfies the conditions of Theorem 2.1, but is not necessarily rational. Then let $x = (1 + \xi^2)^{-1}$ and

$$f(x) = F(\xi) = F(\sqrt{(1/x) - 1}) \qquad (0 < x \leqq 1)$$

with $f(0) = 0$. Then f is continuous on $[0, 1]$ and further

$$g(x) = (f(x) - M)/(1 - x) + M$$

is continuous there also. Next, since $F(\xi) = O(\xi^{-2})$ at infinity, $f(x) = O(x)$ near the origin, and $g(x) = O(x)$ there also. By Lemma 5, for each $\varepsilon > 0$ there are polynomials $g_{\pm\varepsilon}(x)$ such that $g_{\pm\varepsilon}(0) = 0$, $g_{-\varepsilon}(x) \leqq g(x) \leqq g_\varepsilon(x)$ and $|g(x) - g_{\pm\varepsilon}(x)| \leqq \varepsilon$. Then if

$$f_{\pm\varepsilon}(x) = Mx + (1 - x)g_{\pm\varepsilon}(x)$$

the $f_{\pm\varepsilon}$ have the properties (a) $f_{\pm\varepsilon}(0) = 0$, (b) $f_{-\varepsilon}(x) \leqq f(x) \leqq f(x)$ and (c) $|f(x) - f_{\pm\varepsilon}(x)| \leqq \varepsilon(1 - x)$. Now put

$$F_{\pm\varepsilon}(\xi) = f_{\pm\varepsilon}(1/(1 + \xi^2))\,.$$

Then $F_{\pm\varepsilon}(\xi)$ is a rational function such that $(\alpha) F_{\pm\varepsilon}(\xi) \varepsilon L(-\infty, \infty)$, (β) $F_{-\varepsilon}(\xi) \leqq F(\xi) \leqq F_\varepsilon(\xi)$, and (γ) $|F(\xi) - F_{\pm\varepsilon}(\xi)| \leqq \varepsilon(\xi^2/(1 + \xi^2))$. Thus $F_{\pm\varepsilon}(\xi)$ satisfies the hypotheses of Theorem 2.1, and so

$$\lambda_{v,A}(F_{\pm\varepsilon}) = M + F''_{\pm\varepsilon}(0)\pi^2 v^2/8A^2 + o(A^{-2})\,.$$

Since $F_{\pm\varepsilon}(0) = M_0 = F(0)$, condition (γ) shows that $F''_{\pm\varepsilon}(0) \to -\sigma^2$ as $\varepsilon \to 0$, and the Courant-Weyl lemma yields

$$\lambda_{v,A}(F) = M - \sigma^2 \pi^2 v^2/8A^2 + o(A^{-2})$$

completing the proof of the theorem.

2.4 Generalizations

The main theorem proved in the preceding sections was a starting point, rather than a terminal point, of a stream of research in the theory of Toeplitz forms. We summarize here some of the extensions which have been made, though we do not require any of these for our present purposes. First in [49] Widom proved considerably more than Theorem 2.1. Regarding the integral equation (2.1) he determined the next term in the asymptotic expansion of $\lambda_{\nu,A}$,

$$\lambda_{\nu,A} = M - (\sigma^2\pi^2\nu^2/8A^2)[1+\alpha/A] + O(1/A^3) \tag{2.31}$$

under the additional hypothesis that $F^{(iv)}(\xi)$ is continuous at $\xi=0$, where

$$\alpha = \frac{1}{\pi}\int_{-\infty}^{\infty}\frac{1}{\xi^2}\log\left[\frac{2}{\sigma^2}\,\frac{M-F(\xi)}{\xi^2}\right]d\xi\,. \tag{2.32}$$

It is interesting to observe that whereas the first two terms of (2.31) depend only on properties of $F(\xi)$ near $\xi=0$, the next term is global in character.

Again, in [49] the analogues of the above results were proved for Toeplitz *matrices*, rather than integral operators. It was shown that if $f(\theta)$ is continuous and periodic of period 2π, and if $\max f(\theta) = M = f(0)$ and that $\theta=0$ is the only θ (mod 2π) where $f(\theta)=M$; if further f is even, and four times differentiable at $\theta=0$, then, for the νth eigenvalue of the nth section of the Toeplitz matrix associated with $f(\theta)$, we have

$$\lambda_{\nu,n} = M - (\sigma^2\pi^2\gamma^2/2(n+1)^2)[1+\alpha/(n+1)] + o(n^{-3}) \qquad (n\to\infty) \tag{2.33}$$

where

$$\alpha = \frac{1}{2\pi}\int_{-\pi}^{\pi} csc^2\frac{\theta}{2}\log[((M-f(\theta))/2\sigma^2)\cot^2\theta/2]\,d\theta\,. \tag{2.34}$$

In [51] Widom generalized these results to a different behavior of $F(\xi)$ near $\xi=0$. Instead of

$$\lim_{\xi\to 0}(1/\xi^2)(M-F(\xi)) = \sigma^2/2$$

one assumes

$$\lim_{\xi\to 0}(1/|\xi|^\alpha)(M-F(\xi)) = c \tag{2.35}$$

and that the kernel $\varrho(x)$ is a probability density, which requires $0<\alpha\leqq 2$.

It was then shown that

$$\lambda_{\nu,A} = 1 - c/(\lambda_\nu A^\alpha) + o(A^{-\alpha}) \qquad (A\to\infty) \tag{2.36}$$

where $\lambda_1 \geqq \lambda_2 \geqq \ldots$ are the eigenvalues of a kernel $K_\alpha(x, y)$ on the interval $(-1, 1)$, namely of

$$K_\alpha(x, y) = ((\cos \alpha\pi/2)/\Gamma(\alpha))\,|x-y|^{\alpha-1} \max(0, x-y)$$

$$-\frac{\sin \alpha\pi/2}{\pi\Gamma(\alpha)}(1-y^2)^{\alpha/2} \int_{-1}^{x} \frac{(x-t)^{\alpha-1}}{(1-t^2)^{\alpha/2}(t-y)}\,dt\,. \qquad (2.37)$$

In [47] Widom removed the condition $0<\alpha\leqq 2$, and proved that (2.36) holds if ϱ is L_p $(1\leqq p\leqq 2)$, and

$$\max_{|\xi|>\delta} R(\xi) < M \qquad (\delta>0) \qquad (2.38)$$

along with (2.35).

Corresponding results were proved by Parter for Toeplitz matrices. The original result of [26] for $\alpha=2$ was extended to $\alpha=4$ by Parter in [28], to all even integers α in [30], and to all α by Parter in [29]. This last result asserts that if $f(\theta)$ is real, continuous and periodic of period 2π; if $\min f(\theta)=f(0)=0$ is attained only at $\theta=0 \pmod{2\pi}$; further if $[f(\theta)]2^{k/\alpha}=g(\theta)$, where $k=k(\alpha)=$ the smallest integer $\geqq \alpha/2$, and $g(\theta)$ has $2k$ continuous derivatives at $\theta=0$, and $g^{(2k)}(0)=\sigma^2>0$ is the first nonvanishing derivative of g at $\theta=0$, then

$$\lambda_{\nu,n} \sim (1/n^\alpha \lambda_\nu)(\sigma/2k!)^{\alpha/2k} \qquad (n\to\infty) \qquad (2.39)$$

where, again, λ_ν is the νth eigenvalue of $K_\alpha(x, y)$ in (2.37) on $(-1, 1)$ and

$$\lambda_{1,n} \leqq \lambda_{2,n} \leqq \cdots$$

In Ref. [46], Widom unified and greatly extended the scope of the above results by the use of functional analysis rather than the function-theoretic techniques used above. This method, which we shall now describe, is capable of producing the degree of precision which we require, in a much more general setting. Previous methods seem more readily susceptible of yielding additional terms in the asymptotic expansions, in applications where they may be required.

The basic idea of this generalization can readily be illustrated because it consists in replacing the family of problems

$$\lambda\phi(x) = \int_{-A}^{A} K(x-y)\phi(y)\,dy$$

for varying A by

$$\lambda\psi(x) = \int_{-1}^{1} AK(A(x-y))\psi(y)\,dy\,.$$

In itself this is scarcely revolutionary. It suggests, however, that one can profitably think of a family of integral operators on a single compact set $[-1, 1]$, rather than a variable set $[-A, A]$ carrying a fixed kernel. If K_A is the integral operator whose kernel is $AK(A(x-y))$, then we expect that the eigenvalues of K_A will be of the form

$$M - c_\nu/A^2$$

for large A and so there is a good chance that the sequence of operators

$$A^2(M \cdot I - K_A) \qquad (A \to \infty)$$

actually converges, and if so, we can identify the c_ν with the spectrum of the limit operator. It turns out that the method works just as well if we replace the interval $[-A, A]$ by $t\Omega$, where Ω is a fixed subset of E^N, of positive, finite measure, and t is a scalar $(t \to \infty)$.

If Ω is such a set, then $L_2(\Omega)$ is that subspace of $L_2(E^N)$ which consists of functions of support Ω. Further, $\hat{L}_2(\Omega)$ is the set of Fourier transforms of $L_2(\Omega)$. We use the symbol $|\xi|$ for the lenght of a vector ξ in E^N, $\|F\|$ for the $L_2(\Omega)$ norm

$$\|F\| = \int |F(\xi)|^2 d\xi$$

and, if $J(\xi)$ is a nonnegative function, the norm $|||F|||$ is

$$|||F||| = \int [1 + J(\xi)] \, |F(\xi)|^2 d\xi \, .$$

If $\hat{\mathscr{H}}$ is the set of $F \in \hat{L}_2(\Omega)$ such that $|||F||| < \infty$ then evidently $\hat{\mathscr{H}}$ is a Hilbert space in the obvious inner product,

$$\langle F, G \rangle = \int [1 + J(\xi)] F(\xi) \bar{G}(\xi) d\xi \, .$$

Lemma 1. *Let* $\{F_n\}$ *be a sequence of elements of* $\hat{\mathscr{H}}$ *such that* $\|F_n\| = 1$ *(all n) and if*

$$L = \underline{\lim}\, J(\xi)\,,$$
$$L' = \overline{\lim} \int J(\xi) |F_n(\xi)|^2 d\xi$$

then suppose $L' < L$. *Then there is a subsequence* $\{F_{n'}\}$ *which converges weakly in* $\hat{L}_2(\Omega)$ *to some* $F \in \hat{\mathscr{H}}, F \neq 0$. *If* $L = \infty$ *the convergence is strong.*

Proof. First, since all $\|F_n\| = 1$, there is a weakly convergent subsequence $\{F_{n'}\}$, which converges to an F of $\hat{L}_2(\Omega)$. If $L < \infty$ there is an n_0 such that for $n > n_0$

$$\int J(\xi) |F_n(\xi)|^2 d\xi \leqq (1/3)L + (2/3)L'$$

and there is an R such that for $|\xi| \geqq R$,

$$J(\xi) \geqq (2/3)L + (1/3)L' \, .$$

Then for such n,

$$\left(\frac{2}{3}L+\frac{1}{3}L'\right)\int_{|\xi|\geqq R}|F_n(\xi)|^2 d\xi \leqq \int_{|\xi|\geqq R} J(\xi)|F_n(\xi)|^2 d\xi$$
$$\leqq (1/3)L+(2/3)L'$$

and so

$$\int_{|\xi|\leqq R}|F_n(\xi)|^2 d\xi = 1-\int_{|\xi|>R}|F_n(\xi)|^2 d\xi$$
$$\geqq 1-(L+2L')/(2L+L')$$
$$=(L-L')/(2L+L')\,.$$

Now $F_n \in \hat{L}_2(\Omega)$, $F \in \hat{L}_2(\Omega)$ imply $F_n = \hat{f}_n$, $F=\hat{f}$ for some f_n, f in $L_2(\Omega)$. Also, since $\|f_n\|=1$ a subsequence $f_{n'}$ converges weakly to f. Since Ω has finite measure this evidently entails $F_{n'}\to F$ boundedly, pointwise. It follows from the above that

$$\int_{|\xi|\leqq R}|F(\xi)|^2 d\xi \geqq (L-L')/(2L+L')$$

and so that $F \neq 0$. Now since $F_{n'}\to F$ pointwise and the sequence of integrals

$$\int J(\xi)|F_n(\xi)|^2 d\xi$$

is uniformly bounded, Fatou's lemma implies that $F\in\hat{\mathscr{H}}$. If $L=\infty$, a slight alteration of this argument yields the strong convergence which was claimed.

Now, for the Hilbert space $\hat{\mathscr{H}}$, let $\hat{\mathscr{H}}_0$ be the closure of $\hat{\mathscr{H}}$ in $\hat{L}_2(\Omega)$, the closure being in the norm $\|\ \|$, and let $\mathscr{H}, \mathscr{H}_0$ be the spaces of Fourier transforms of elements of $\hat{\mathscr{H}}, \hat{\mathscr{H}}_0$. For a given $F\in\hat{L}_2(\Omega)$ consider the mapping which sends $G\in\hat{\mathscr{H}}$ into (F, G). It is easy to check that this is a bounded linear functional on $\hat{\mathscr{H}}$, and so it can be represented as an inner product on $\hat{\mathscr{H}}$, namely

$$(F, G) = \langle \hat{B}F, G\rangle$$

defines the operator $\hat{B}$, and we have

$$\|\hat{B}F\| \leqq |||\hat{B}F||| \leqq \|F\|\,.$$

The restriction of $\hat{B}$, defined on all of $\hat{L}_2(\Omega)$, to $\hat{\mathscr{H}}_0$, is a bounded operator on $\hat{\mathscr{H}}_0$ of norm $\leqq 1$, and is self-adjoint.

We define the operator $\hat{A}$ by

$$\hat{A}=\hat{B}^{-1}-I$$

and finally the operator A by inversion of the Fourier transform. That is, Af is the function whose transform is $\hat{A}\hat{f}$. For instance, in one dimension, if $\Omega=[-1,1]$, and $J(\xi)=\xi^2$, Af is the function whose transform is $J(\xi)\hat{f}(\xi)=\xi^2\hat{f}(\xi)$, whence $Af=f''$. We have now associated with each nonnegative $J(\xi)\not\equiv 0$ an operator A which is self-adjoint and whose domain is the set of transforms of functions in the range of $\hat{B}$. If this latter range is $\hat{\mathscr{D}}$, then we call the domain of $A\mathscr{D}$.

Lemma 2. *Let $L=\underline{\lim}\,J(\xi)$, and let $\lambda<L$ be in the spectrum of A. Then λ is an eigenvalue of A of finite multiplicity. Further, the only possible cluster point of these eigenvalues $<L$ is L itself.*

Proof. Let $\lambda<L$ belong to the spectrum of A. Then there is a sequence $\{F_m\}\in\hat{\mathscr{D}}$ such that

$$\|(\hat{A}-\lambda I)F_m\|\to 0\,.$$

We can suppose the F_m normalized to $\|F_m\|=1$. Now from the definition of $\hat{B}$

$$(F,G)=\langle\hat{B}F,G\rangle \qquad (F\in\hat{L}_2(\Omega),\, G\in\hat{\mathscr{H}})$$

we have

$$\int F(\xi)\overline{G(\xi)}d\xi=\int(1+J(\xi))\hat{B}F(\xi)\bar{G}(\xi)d\xi\,.$$

Putting $\hat{B}F(\xi)=F_1(\xi)\in\hat{\mathscr{D}}$

$$\int(\hat{A}+I)F_1(\xi)\overline{G(\xi)}d\xi=\int(1+J(\xi))F_1(\xi)\bar{G}(\xi)d\xi$$

or finally

$$\int J(\xi)F(\xi)\overline{G(\xi)}d\xi=\int\hat{A}F(\xi)\overline{G(\xi)}d\xi$$

for all $F\in\hat{\mathscr{D}}$, $G\in\hat{\mathscr{H}}$. In particular,

$$\begin{aligned}\int J(\xi)|F_m(\xi)|^2d\xi&=\int\hat{A}F_m(\xi)\overline{F_m(\xi)}d\xi\\&=\int(\lambda F_m(\xi)+\varepsilon_m(\xi))\overline{F_m(\xi)}d\xi\end{aligned}$$

where $\|\varepsilon_m(\xi)\|\to 0$, and so

$$\int J(\xi)|F_m(\xi)|^2d\xi=\lambda+o(1)\qquad(m\to\infty)\,.$$

Since $\lambda<L$, Lemma 1 yields at once a subsequence $F_{m'}$ which converges weakly to an F of $\hat{\mathscr{H}}$, $F\neq 0$. We claim that this F is an eigenvector of $\hat{A}$. Indeed, let $G\in\hat{\mathscr{D}}$, then

$$\begin{aligned}\lambda(F,G)&=\lim\lambda(F_{m'}G)=\lim(\hat{A}F_{m'},G)\\&=\lim(F_{m'},\hat{A}G)\\&=(F,\hat{A}G)\\&=(\hat{A}F,G)\,.\end{aligned}$$

Hence $(\hat{A}F-\lambda F,G)=0$ for all $G\in\hat{\mathscr{D}}$, establishing the claim. If there were a cluster point $\lambda<L$ of these eigenvalues there would be a sequence

$\{\lambda_n\}$ of eigenvalues and $\{F_n\}$ of eigenvectors such that $\lambda_n \to \lambda$ and $F_n \to 0$ weakly, contradicting Lemma 1.

We have defined, corresponding to a nonnegative function $J(\xi)$, an operator A. We want to show that if, in a suitable sense, we have a family of functions $J_t(\xi)$ converging to $J(\xi)$ then the corresponding operators A_t converge to A. Regarding the suitable sense in which the functions $J_t(\xi)$ converge to $J(\xi)$ we assume

(H1) $\lim_{t\to\infty} J_t(\xi) = J(\xi)$ *a.e.*

(H2) We have $J_t(\xi) \leqq c_1 + c_2 J(\xi)$ for all t, ξ.

(H3) If $\varepsilon > 0$ is given, there is an $R > 0$ and a $t_0 > 0$ such that

$$J_t(\xi) \geqq \begin{cases} L-\varepsilon & L<\infty \\ \varepsilon^{-1} & L=\infty \end{cases}$$

for all $t \geqq t_0$, $|\xi| \geqq R$.

Now we let $\hat{\mathscr{H}}, \hat{\mathscr{H}}_0, \hat{\mathscr{D}}$ be the spaces corresponding to the function $J(\xi)$ and $\hat{\mathscr{H}}_t, \hat{\mathscr{H}}_{0t}, \hat{\mathscr{D}}_t$ be those for the functions $J_t(\xi)$.

Lemma 3. *Let* $F_t \in \hat{\mathscr{H}}_t$, *suppose* (H1)–(H3) *and that* $\|F_t\| = 1$, $\overline{\lim_t} \int J_t(\xi)|F_t(\xi)|^2 d\xi < L$. *Then there is a subsequence* $F_{t'}$, *an* $F \varepsilon \hat{\mathscr{H}}$, $F \neq 0$ *such that* $F_{t'} \to F$ *weakly. If* $L = \infty$ *the convergence is strong.*

Proof. As in Lemma 1.

Lemma 4. *Let* $F_t \in \hat{\mathscr{H}}_t$, *suppose* (H1)–(H3), *that* $F_{t'} \to F$ *weakly and that*

$$\int J_t(\xi)|F_t(\xi)|^2 d\xi = O(1) \qquad (t\to\infty).$$

Then

$$\int J_t(\xi)F_t(\xi)\bar{G}(\xi)d\xi \to \int J(\xi)F(\xi)\overline{G(\xi)}d\xi$$

for all $G \in \hat{\mathscr{H}}$.

Proof. The sequence of functions $J_t(\xi)^{1/2}F_t(\xi)$ has uniformly bounded norms, hence has a weakly convergent subsequence. However, $J_t^{1/2} \to J^{1/2}$ pointwise and $F_t \to F$ pointwise, and so $J_t^{1/2} \to J^{1/2}F$ weakly. Furthermore, for $G \in \hat{\mathscr{H}}$

$$\|GJ^{1/2} - GJ_t^{1/2}\|^2 = \int |G(\xi)^2 (J_t(\xi)^{1/2} - J(\xi)^{1/2})^2 d\xi$$

which converges to zero by (H2) and the dominated convergence theorem, and the result follows.

Lemma 5. *Under* (H1)–(H3), *for all* $t > t_0$ *the spectrum of* A_t *is disjoint from any preassigned closed interval which is to the left of* L *and disjoint from the spectrum of* A.

Proof. If false there is a sequence of $t\to\infty$ and a sequence λ_t each belonging to such an interval I and to the spectrum of A_t. Now, by (H3), I is to the left of $L_t = \underline{\lim}\, J_t$ for $t > t_0$, and by Lemma 2, the λ_t are eigenvalues of the A_t. Let F_t be the normalized eigenfunction of $\hat{A}_t$ for the eigenvalue λ_t. By Lemma 3, a subsequence $F_{t'}$ converges weakly to some $F \neq 0$ of $\hat{\mathscr{H}}$, and by refinement, we can suppose $\lambda_t \to \lambda$. By Lemma 4 with $G \in \hat{\mathscr{D}}$,

$$\begin{aligned}\lambda(F,G) &= \lim \lambda_{t'}(F_{t'},G)\\ &= \lim(\hat{A}F_{t'},G)\\ &= \lim(F_{t'},\hat{A}G)\\ &= (F,\hat{A}G) \qquad (\text{all } G\in\hat{\mathscr{D}}).\end{aligned}$$

Hence $F\in\hat{\mathscr{D}}$, $\hat{A}F-\lambda F=0$, λ is an eigenvalue of $\hat{A}$, and we have a contradiction to the fact that λ lies in the interval I.

We can now prove the main result which asserts the convergence of the spectral families of projections $E_t(\lambda)$ corresponding to the operators A_t to the family $E(\lambda)$ belonging to A. Here strong convergence of operators means that

$$\|(E_t(\lambda)-E(\lambda))f\| \to 0 \qquad (t\to\infty)$$

for all $f\in\mathscr{H}_0$, while uniform convergence means that

$$\|(E_t(\lambda)-E(\lambda))f\| \leqq \varepsilon_t \|f\|$$

for some constants $\varepsilon_t \to 0$, for all $f\in\mathscr{H}_0$, the ε_t being independent of f. Then we have

Lemma 6. *Assume* (H1)–(H3). *If* $\lambda < L$ *and* λ *is not an eigenvalue of* A, *then* $\{E_t(\lambda)\}\to E(\lambda)$ *in the strong topology on* $\mathscr{H}_0$. *If* $L=\infty$ *we have convergence in the uniform topology.*

Proof. By the Cauchy integral formula for operators,

$$\hat{E}(\lambda) = (1/2\pi i)\int_C (\hat{A}-zI)^{-1}\,dz$$

where C can be chosen, say, as a circle centered at $\lambda/2$, of radius λ. By Lemma 5, C is disjoint from the spectrum of $\hat{A}_t$ for $t>t_0$, so

$$\hat{E}_t(\lambda) = (1/2\pi i)\int_C (\hat{A}_t-zI)^{-1}\,dz$$

with the same contour C.

We claim that

$$(\hat{A}_t - zI)^{-1} \to (\hat{A}-zI)^{-1} \qquad (t\to\infty)$$

weakly.

Indeed, let $F \in \mathscr{H}_0$. Then from the identity

$$Q(Q-zI)^{-1} = I + z(Q-zI)^{-1}$$

with $Q = \hat{A}_t$ we get

$$\hat{A}_t(\hat{A}_t - zI)^{-1}F = F + z(\hat{A}_t - zI)^{-1}F \tag{2.40}$$

from which

$$\int J_t(\xi)|(\hat{A}_t - zI)^{-1}F(\xi)|^2 d\xi = (\hat{A}(\hat{A}_t - zI)^{-1}F, (\hat{A}_t - zI)^{-1}F).$$

For $z \in C$, the operators $(\hat{A}_t - zI)^{-1}$ are uniformly bounded, for $t > t_0$, because the contour C is bounded away from the spectrum of A_t. Hence

$$\int J_t(\xi)|(\hat{A}_t - zI)^{-1}F(\xi)|^2 d\xi$$

is uniformly bounded in t. Then by Lemma 3 there is a subsequence $\{t'\}$ on which $(\hat{A}_{t'} - zI)^{-1}F$ converges weakly to some H. By Lemma 4, if $G \in \hat{\mathscr{D}}$,

$$(\hat{A}_{t'}(\hat{A}_{t'} - zI)^{-1}F, G) \to (H, \hat{A}G)$$

and by (2.40)

$$(H, \hat{A}G) = (F, G) + z(H, G).$$

Since $\hat{A}$ is self-adjoint, $H \in \hat{\mathscr{D}}$ and $(\hat{A} - zI)H = F$ or

$$H = (\hat{A} - zI)^{-1}F.$$

Thus each sequence of t has a subsequence along which

$$(\hat{A}_{t'} - zI)^{-1}F \to (\hat{A} - zI)^{-1}F$$

weakly and so $(\hat{A}_t - zI)^{-1}F$ itself converges weakly to $(\hat{A} - zI)^{-1}F$, as claimed. Then from the Cauchy formula $\hat{E}_t(\lambda)$ converges weakly to $\hat{E}(\lambda)$ and therefore strongly also, proving the first assertion of the lemma.

If $L = \infty$ and the convergence were not uniform there would be $F_t \in \hat{\mathscr{H}}$ of norm 1, and $\delta > 0$ for which

$$\|\hat{E}_t(\lambda)F_t - \hat{E}(\lambda)F_t\| \geqq \delta.$$

Then by Lemma 3 there would be a subsequence of t along which $\hat{E}_t(\lambda)F_t$ and $\hat{E}(\lambda)F_t$ both converge strongly, say to G_1 and G_2. Then $\|G_1 - G_2\| \geqq \delta$, but $G_1 = G_2$ since $\hat{E}_t(\lambda) \to \hat{E}(\lambda)$ weakly, a contradiction.

The general form of Widom's theorem on the eigenvalues of integral kernels is now in hand. It is

Theorem 2.2. *Let $k(x)$ be $L_1(E_N)$, let $k(x) = \overline{k(-x)}$, and put*

$$K(\xi) = \int e^{-i\xi \cdot x} k(x) dx.$$

Suppose that $M = K(0) > 0$, that for each $\delta > 0$

$$\max_{\substack{|\xi_i| \geqq \delta \\ \text{all } i}} K(\xi) < M$$

and that for $\xi \to 0$ *we have*

$$K(\xi) = M - |\xi|^\alpha \Phi(\xi/|\xi|) + O(|\xi|^\alpha)$$

where α *is positive and* $0 < \Delta_1 \leqq \phi(\xi) \leqq \Delta_2 < \infty$ *for* $|\xi| = 1$. *Let*

$$\mu_{1,t} \geqq \mu_{2,t} \geqq \dots$$

be the positive eigenvalues of $A_{K(\xi/t)}$, *and let*

$$\lambda_1 \leqq \lambda_2 \leqq \dots$$

be the eigenvalues of $A_{J(\xi)}$, *where* $J(\xi) = |\xi|^\alpha \Phi(\xi/|\xi|)$. *Then for each fixed m,*

$$\mu_{m,t} = M - \lambda_m/t^\alpha + o(t^{-\alpha}) \qquad (t \to \infty).$$

Proof. Take

$$J(\xi) = |\xi|^\alpha \Phi(\xi/|\xi|),$$
$$J_t(\xi) = t^\alpha [M - K(\xi/t)]$$

in Lemma 6.

2.5 Hilbert's Inequality Revisited

Using Widom's theorem, as well as an independent method, we can now determine more precisely the asymptotic behavior of the eigenvales of sections of the Hilbert matrix. We follow de Bruijn and Wilf [11]. Consider first the associated integral problem

$$\Lambda_n f(u) = \int_1^n (f(v)/(u+v))dv. \tag{2.41}$$

Make the substitution

$$\begin{aligned} f(u) = u^{-1/2} g(u); \quad n = e^{2A}; \quad u = e^{x+A}; \\ v = e^{y+A}; \quad g(e^{x+A}) = \phi(x). \end{aligned} \tag{2.42}$$

Then (2.41) takes the form

$$\Lambda_n \phi(x) = \int_{-A}^{A} K(x-y)\phi(y)dy \tag{2.43}$$

where we have put

$$K(t) \;\; 1/(2\cosh t/2). \tag{2.44}$$

The problem (2.42) is of the precise form considered in Theorem 2.1 where the Fourier transform is

$$F(\xi) = \int_{-\infty}^{\infty} e^{i\xi t} K(t)dt = \pi/\cosh \pi\xi \tag{2.45}$$
$$= \pi - \pi^3 \xi^2/2 + O(\xi^4).$$

Hence from Theorem 2.1 with $\sigma^2=\pi^3$, $A=(1/2)\log n$ we find

$$\Lambda_n=\pi-\pi^5/2(\log n)^2+O((\log n)^{-3}) \tag{2.46}$$

for the largest eigenvalue of (2.43), and indeed

$$\Lambda_{n,v}=\pi-\pi^5 v^2/2(\log n)^2+O((\log n)^{-3}) \tag{2.47}$$

for the vth eigenvalue.

We give another proof of (2.46). From the identity

$$\int_{-\infty}^{\infty}\frac{1}{2\cosh(x-y)/2}\cos ty\,dy=\left(\frac{\pi}{\cosh\pi t}\right)\cos tx \tag{2.48}$$

one finds that

$$\phi^{(1)}(x)=\cos\pi x/2A$$

is an eigenfunction of the problem

$$\int_{-\infty}^{\infty}K(x-y)\phi(y)dy=\Lambda\phi(x)$$

corresponding to the eigenvalue

$$\Lambda_n^{(1)}=\pi/(\cosh\pi^2/2A)\,.$$

Also from (2.48), the function

$$\phi^{(2)}(x)=\cos\pi x/2(A+p)$$

is an eigenfunction of the same problem with eigenvalue

$$\Lambda_n^{(2)}=\pi/(\cosh\pi^2/2(A+p))\,.$$

Now, for $-A\leqq x\leqq A$, we assert that

$$\int_A^{\infty}K(x-y)\phi^{(1)}(y)dy<0 \tag{2.49}$$

for the left side is

$$\begin{aligned}\int_A^{\infty}K(x-y)(\cos\pi y/2A)dy&=\sum_{m=1}^{\infty}\int_{(2m-1)A}^{(2m+1)A}K(x-y)(\cos\pi y/2A)dy\\ &=\sum_{m=1}^{\infty}\int_{-1}^{1}K(x-A(2m+t))\left(\cos\frac{\pi}{2}(2m+t)\right)A\,dt\\ &=A\sum_{m-1}^{\infty}(-1)^m\int_{-1}^{1}K(x-A(2m+t))\cos\frac{\pi t}{2}\,dt\,.\end{aligned} \tag{2.50}$$

This is an alternating series, of negative first term, whose terms decrease steadily in magnitude, which establishes (2.49). In a similar way we can show that

$$\int_{-\infty}^{-A} K(x-y)\phi^{(1)}(y)dy<0 \quad (|x|\leqq A). \tag{2.51}$$

Next, by similar reasoning we have, for $|x|\leqq A$,

$$\begin{aligned}\int_{A}^{\infty} K(x-y)\phi^{(2)}(y)dy &= \int_{A}^{\infty} K(x-y)(\cos\pi y/2(A+p))dy\\ &> \int_{A}^{3(A+p)} K(x-y)(\cos\pi y/2(A+p))dy\\ &> \int_{A}^{3(A+p)} e^{-|x-y|/2}(\cos\pi y/2(A+p))dy\\ &\sim e^{(x-A)/2}\pi(p-1)/2A \quad (A\to\infty)\end{aligned}$$

where the last estimate is valid if $p>1$ and $p=o(A)$. Hence for such p,

$$\int_{A}^{\infty} K(x-y)\phi^{(2)}(y)dy>0 \quad (|x|\leqq A) \tag{2.52}$$

and the same for $\int_{-\infty}^{-A}$. It follows that

$$\begin{aligned}\int_{-A}^{A} K(x-y)\phi^{(1)}(y)dy &= \int_{-\infty}^{\infty} - \int_{A}^{\infty} - \int_{-\infty}^{-A}\\ &\geqq \int_{-\infty}^{\infty}\\ &= \Lambda_n^{(1)}\phi^{(1)}(x)\end{aligned}$$

and

$$\begin{aligned}\int_{-A}^{A} K(x-y)\phi^{(2)}(y)dy &= \int_{-\infty}^{\infty} - \int_{A}^{\infty} - \int_{-\infty}^{-A}\\ &\leqq \int_{-\infty}^{\infty}\\ &= \Lambda_n^{(2)}\phi^{(2)}(x).\end{aligned}$$

From the Perron-Frobenius theory of positive kernels of follows that

$$\Lambda_n^{(1)}\leqq\Lambda_n\leqq\Lambda_n^{(2)}$$

and (2.46) follows at once.

By either of these two methods, we arrive at the expansion (2.46) for the largest eigenvalue of the integral problem (2.41). It remains to determine this behavior for the matrix problem

$$\lambda_n x_\mu = \sum_{\nu=1}^{n} x_\nu/(\mu+\nu) \qquad (\mu=1, \ldots, n). \tag{2.53}$$

The method consists in relating λ_n to Λ_n. Indeed, for $1 \leqq u, v \leqq n+1$,

$$1/(u+v) \leqq 1/([u]+[v]). \tag{2.54}$$

Hence the largest eigenvalue of the kernel on the left is not greater than the largest eigenvalue of the kernel on the right. But this latter eigenvalue is λ_n, for if x is an eigenvector of (2.35) put $\psi(v) = x_\mu$ for $\mu \leqq v < \mu+1$, and then

$$\lambda\psi(u) = \int_1^{n+1} (\psi(v)/([u]+[v]))dv \qquad (1 \leqq u \leqq n+1).$$

Thus $\Lambda_{n+1} \leqq \lambda_n$.

Let $h>0$. Then

$$1/([u]+[v]) \leqq (1+h)/(u+v-2+2h) \qquad (1 \leqq u, v \leqq n+1)$$

and so $\lambda_n \leqq \lambda_n^{(1)}$ where $\lambda_n^{(1)}$ is the largest eigenvalue of the kernel

$$(1+h)/(u+v-2+2h)$$

on the interval $(1, n+1)$. By a change of variable, one sees that $\lambda_n^{(1)} = \lambda_n^{(2)}$, where $\lambda_n^{(2)}$ is the largest eigenvalue of

$$(1+h)/(u+v)$$

on the interval $(h, n+h)$, and $\lambda_n^{(2)} = (1+h)\lambda_n^{(3)}$, where $\lambda_n^{(3)}$ is the largest eigenvalue of the kernel

$$1/(u+\mathrm{v})$$

on the interval $\left(1, 1+\dfrac{n}{h}\right)$.

But we are now back to the original kernel on a different interval, and so

$$\lambda_n^{(3)} = (1+h)(\pi - \pi^5/8A_1^2 + O(A_1^{-3}))$$

where

$$A_1 = (1/2)\log(n+h)/h.$$

If we put

$$h = \left(\frac{1}{2}\log n\right)^{-3}$$

we obtain

Theorem 2.2. *The best possible constant for the inequality*

$$\sum_{\mu,\nu=1}^{n} x_\mu x_\nu/(\mu+\nu) \leqq \lambda_n \sum_{\mu=1}^{n} x_\mu^2 \tag{2.55}$$

is of the form

$$\lambda_n = \pi - \pi^5/2(\log n)^2 + O((\log\log n)/(\log n)^3) \qquad (n\to\infty). \tag{2.56}$$

2.6 Homogeneous Kernels of Degree — 1

This method carries over without substantial change to kernels $K(x, y)$ which are homogeneous of degree -1, symmetric, and decreasing (Wilf [54]). In that case, the same substitution (2.42) transforms the problem

$$\Lambda_n f(u) = \int_1^n K(u, v) f(v) dv \tag{2.57}$$

into

$$\Lambda_n g(u) = \int_{-A}^{A} G(u-v) g(v) dv \tag{2.58}$$

where, corresponding to (2.44),

$$G(u) = K(e^{u/2}, e^{-u/2}) \tag{2.59}$$

and is even, by symmetry of K. Application of Widom's theorem 2.1 yields

$$\Lambda_n = M - \pi^2\gamma/(\log n)^2 + O((\log n)^{-3}) \qquad (n\to\infty) \tag{2.60}$$

where

$$M = \int_0^\infty K(t, 1) t^{-1/2} dt \tag{2.61}$$

is identical with M of (1.11) and

$$\gamma = \int_1^\infty (\log t)^2 K(t, 1) t^{-1/2} dt\,. \tag{2.62}$$

To relate Λ_n to λ_n we also proceed as before, getting $K([u],[v]) \geqq K(u, v)$ and $\lambda_n \geqq \Lambda_{n+1}$, and then

$$\begin{aligned}(1+h)K(u-1+h, v-1+h) &= K((u-1+h)/(1+h), (v-1+h)/(1+h))\\ &\geqq K([u],[v])\end{aligned}$$

leads through $\lambda_n^{(1)}, \lambda_n^{(2)}, \lambda_n^{(3)}$ just as above to

Theorem 2.3. *Let $K(x\ y)$ be symmetric, homogeneous of degree* -1, *and decreasing. Let*

$$K(1,t)=O(t^{-(1/2)-\delta}) \qquad (t\to\infty)$$

for some $\delta>0$. Let λ_n be the best possible constant for the inequality

$$\sum_{\mu,\nu=1}^{n} K(\mu,\nu)x_\mu x_\nu \leqq \lambda_n \sum_{\mu=1}^{n} x_\mu^2 . \tag{2.63}$$

Then, as $n\to\infty$, we have

$$\lambda_n = M-\pi^2\gamma/(\log n)^2+O((\log\log n)/(\log n)^3) . \tag{2.64}$$

This theorem constitutes a refinement of Theorem 1.1 to n variables, and, incidentally, shows that the constant M of that theorem was best possible. As an application of the theorem, take

$$K(x,y)=1/(\max(x,y)) . \tag{2.65}$$

Then $M=4$, $\gamma=16$, and the best constant for the inequality

$$\sum_{\mu,\nu=1}^{n} x_\mu x_\nu/\max(\mu,\nu) \leqq \lambda_n \sum_{\mu=1}^{n} x_\mu^2 \tag{2.66}$$

is

$$\lambda_n = 4-16\pi^2/(\log n)^2+O((\log\log n)/(\log n)^3) \qquad (n\to\infty). \tag{2.67}$$

Again, for Hardy's inequality in l^2.

$$\sum_{\nu=1}^{n} ((a_1+\cdots+a_\nu)/\nu)^2 \leqq \lambda_n \sum_{\nu=1}^{n} a_\nu^2 \tag{2.68}$$

the coefficient matrix is

$$A=(a_{\mu\nu})=\begin{cases}1/\mu^2+\cdots+1/n^2 & (\nu\leqq\mu)\\ 1/\nu^2+\cdots+1/n^2 & (\nu\geqq\mu)\end{cases}$$

and this is not homogeneous of degree -1. However, if we write

$$B=(DE)A(DE)^{-1}$$

where

$$E_{ij}=\begin{cases}1 & i\geqq j\\ 0 & i<j\end{cases} \qquad D_{ij}=i^{-1}\delta_{ij}$$

we find that

$$B_{\mu\nu}=1/(\max(\mu,\nu) .$$

Since B is similar to A, λ_n of (2.68) is identical with λ_n of (2.66), and so (2.67) holds in (2.68) as well.

Consider again the relationship between the homogeneous kernels of degree -1 and the Toeplitz kernels. Eqs. (2.57) and (2.58) show that the integral kernels

(I) $K(u, v)$, K symmetric and homogeneous of degree -1, on $[1, n]$ and

(II) $G(u-v)$, $G(t)$ even, on $[-\frac{1}{2}\log n, \frac{1}{2}\log n]$ where

$$G(u) = K(e^{u/2}, e^{-u/2}) \tag{2.69}$$

have the same spectra. Conversely, given the Toeplitz kernel $G(u-v)$ on $(-A, A)$, the kernel $K(u, v)$ is

$$K(u, v) = (1/\sqrt{uv})G(\log u/v) \tag{2.70}$$

on the interval $[1, e^{2n}]$. It is evidently homogeneous, and if G is even, it is symmetric also. Here are certain other facets of this dual relationship (Wilf [53]).

a) Fourier Transform. The spectral theory of Toeplitz kernels is determined by the behavior of the Fourier transform of the kernel $G(u)$. If $G(u)$ is given by (2.69), then its Fourier transform is

$$\begin{aligned} F(\xi) &= \int_{-\infty}^{\infty} e^{iu\xi} K(e^{u/2}, e^{-u/2}) du \\ &= \int_0^{\infty} t^{-1+i\xi} K(t^{1/2}, t^{-1/2}) dt \\ &= \int_0^{\infty} t^{-(1/2)+i\xi} K(t, 1) dt \\ &= \int_0^{\infty} t^{-s} K(t, 1) dt \end{aligned} \tag{2.71}$$

where $s = 1/2 + i\xi$ and the homogeneity of K was used in the second transformation of the integral. The behavior of $F(\xi)$ on the *real line* is equivalent to the behavior of

$$\mathcal{J}(s) = \int_0^{\infty} t^{-s} K(t, 1) dt, \tag{2.72}$$

the Mellin transform of $K(t, 1)$ on the *critical line* ($\operatorname{Re} s = 1/2$) in the complex plane. At this point the reader may wish to look back at the bound (1.11) which appears in such an artifical way in Theorem 1.1. In view of the present discussion that bound M is just $\mathcal{J}(1/2)$ which is, after a rotation, the Fourier transform of a Toeplitz kernel at the origin, a very natural bound.

b) Spectral Density. The analogue of (1.33) is well known to hold for integral operators (Kac, Murdock, and Szegö [26]), namely if $N_A(a, b)$ is the number of eigenvalues of the problem

$$\lambda\phi(u) = \int_{-A}^{A} G(u-v)\phi(v)dv \tag{2.73}$$

which lie in the interval (a, b), where $0 < a < b \leqq M$ then

$$\lim_{A\to\infty} N_A(a, b)/2A = (1/\pi)\times \text{ measure } \quad \{\xi \mid a < F(\xi) < b\}$$

where F is the Fourier transform of G and $M = F(0)$. It is now easy to translate this into a theorem about homogeneous kernels of degree -1. Indeed if $K(x, y)$ is such a kernel, and if $f_n(\theta)$ denotes the number of eigenvalues of the problem

$$\lambda\phi(u) = \int_{1}^{n} K(u, v)\phi(v)dv \tag{2.74}$$

which lie in the interval $(\theta M, M)$ then

$$f_n(\theta) \sim H(\theta)\log n \qquad (n\to\infty) \tag{2.75}$$

for each fixed θ, where

$$H(\theta) = \frac{1}{\pi} \times \text{ measure } \left\{\xi \,\middle|\, \theta M < \mathscr{F}\left(\frac{1}{2} + i\xi\right) < M\right\} \tag{2.76}$$

and $M = \mathscr{F}(1/2)$.

For example, take $K(x, y) = (x+y)^{-1}$, the Hilbert kernel. Then $\mathscr{J}(s) = \csc \pi s$ $(0 < \operatorname{Re} s < 1)$. If $f_n(\theta)$ is the number of eigenvalues of the Hilbert kernel which lie in $(\theta\pi, \pi)$ then

$$f_n(\theta) \sim \left(\frac{2}{\pi}\cosh^{-1} 1/\theta\right)\log n \qquad (n\to\infty)\,. \tag{2.77}$$

This estimate for the spectral density, proved for the Hilbert integral operator, actually holds also for the Hilbert matrix. This cannot be proved by appeal to duality, but requires special methods, which we will discuss in Section 3.6.

c) Representation Theorem. A quadratic form in a Toeplitz matrix is representable as the mean square of a trigonometric polynomial, as in (1.29).

We investigate the corresponding question for homogeneous kernels. Given $K(u, v)$ we define its Mellin transform by (2.72), and we suppose K to be decreasing, symmetric, continuous in both arguments jointly, and homogeneous of degree -1. Then $\mathscr{F}(s)$ is analytic in the strip

$0 < \operatorname{Re} s < 1$. It is also easy to verify that it satisfies the functional equation

$$\mathscr{F}(s) = \mathscr{F}(1-s) \tag{2.78}$$

in that strip. By the Mellin inversion formula ([41], p. 46), valid if $t^{-1/2}K(1,t)$ is $\mathscr{L}(0,\infty)$,

$$K(t,1) = (1/2\pi) \int_{-\infty}^{\infty} \mathscr{F}(1/2 + i\xi) t^{-(1/2)-i\xi} d\xi$$

and so

$$\begin{aligned} K(u,v) &= v^{-1} K(u/v, 1) \\ &= \frac{1}{2\pi} \int_{-\infty}^{\infty} \mathscr{F}(1/2 + i\xi) u^{-(1/2)-i\xi} v^{-(1/2)+i\xi} d\xi . \end{aligned} \tag{2.79}$$

Let $x_1, x_2, \ldots$ be a sequence of complex numbers. Then we obtain from (2.79) the representation theorem for quadratic forms in such kernels, namely

$$\sum_{1 \leq \mu, \nu \leq n} K(\mu, \nu) \overline{x_\mu} x_\nu = \frac{1}{2\pi} \int_{-\infty}^{\infty} \mathscr{F}\left(\frac{1}{2} + i\xi\right) \left| \sum_{\nu=1}^{n} \frac{x_\nu}{\nu^{\frac{1}{2}+i\xi}} \right|^2 d\xi . \tag{2.80}$$

This is the analogue of (1.29). We see that the Mellin transform on the critical line plays the role of the Fourier transform on the real axis and a finite Dirichlet series plays the role of the trigonometric polynomial.

These results are evidently related to analytic number theory. If we choose $x_\nu = \nu^{-1/2}$ $(\nu = 1, 2, \ldots)$ and $K(x,y) = \max(x,y)^{-1}$ then (2.80) reads

$$\sum_{1 \leq \mu, \nu \leq n} \frac{1}{\sqrt{\mu\nu} \max(\mu, \nu)} = \frac{1}{2\pi} \int_{-\infty}^{\infty} \frac{1}{(\xi^2 + 1/4)} \left| \sum_{\nu=1}^{n} \frac{1}{\nu^{1+i\xi}} \right|^2 d\xi . \tag{2.81}$$

The sum on the right is a partial sum of the Riemann zeta function on $\operatorname{Re} s = 1$. Since the quadratic form is bounded, we obtain

$$\frac{1}{2\pi} \int_{-\infty}^{\infty} \frac{d\xi}{\xi^2 + 1/4} \left| \sum_{\nu=1}^{n} 1/\nu^{1+i\xi} \right|^2 d\xi = O(\log n) \qquad (n \to \infty) \tag{2.82}$$

a mean value theorem for the partial sums. In general, under our hypotheses, we shall always have

$$\begin{aligned} &(1/2\pi) \int_{-\infty}^{\infty} \mathscr{F}(1/2 + i\xi) \left| \sum_{\nu=1}^{n} x_\nu / \nu^{(1/2)+i\xi} \right|^2 d\xi \\ &\leq \mathscr{F}(1/2) \sum_{\nu=1}^{n} |x_\nu|^2 . \end{aligned} \tag{2.83}$$

CHAPTER III

Hankel Forms

3.1 Introduction

In the preceding chapter we studied kernels of the special forms $K(u-v)$ and $K(\alpha x, \alpha y) = \alpha^{-1} K(x, y)$. Here we consider matrices H of the type

$$H_{ij} = \alpha_{i+j} \qquad (i, j = 0, 1, 2, \ldots).$$

Such matrices, in which the entries depend only on the sum of the subscripts, we call Hankel matrices. They occur as the natural objects of study in moment problems on the real axis (see [36]). For example, a sequence of numbers $\{\mu_n\}_0^\infty$ is called a moment sequence if there exists a bounded non-decreasing function $\psi(x)$ such that

$$\mu_n = \int_{-\infty}^{\infty} t^n \, d\alpha(t) \qquad (n = 0, 1, 2, \ldots). \tag{3.1}$$

For a given sequence $\{\mu_n\}$, how can we tell if such an $\alpha(t)$ exists, or if it is unique? If $\{x_r\}$ is an arbitrary sequence then evidently

$$\sum_{r,s=0}^{n} \bar{x}_r \mu_{r+s} x_s = \int_{-\infty}^{\infty} \left| \sum_{r=0}^{n} x_r t^r \right|^2 d\alpha(t).$$

Hence if such an α exists, then the matrix $\mu_{r+s}]_{r,s=0}^{\infty}$ is nonnegative definite. It turns out that the necessary and sufficient condition for the existence of such an $\alpha(t)$, which does not reduce to a finite set of mass-points, is that the matrix $\mu_{r+s}]_0^\infty$ be positive definite. In other words, if $\{\lambda_N\}_0^\infty$ is the sequence of smallest eigenvalues of the Nth finite sections of the infinite matrix then

$$\lambda_N > 0 \qquad (N = 0, 1, \ldots) \tag{3.2}$$

is the required condition.

Many variations of the moment problem (3.1) have been discussed. In all cases the relevant information for existence of a solution concerns the behavior of the sequence $\{\lambda_N\}$ of smallest eigenvalues of sections of certain Hankel matrices. In keeping with the philosophy of this monograph, we think of (3.2) as a "first-round" inequality, and we will, in this chapter, determine much more precise information about the $\{\lambda_N\}$

of a Hankel matrix of moments. Indeed, the exact asymptotic behavior of the $\{\lambda_N\}$ will be found under very mild hypotheses.

If $\alpha(x)$ is Lebesgue measure on $[0, 1]$, the μ_n of (3.1) are $\mu_n = (n+1)^{-1}$ and so the associated Hankel matrix is

$$\mu_{r+s} = 1/(r+s+1) \qquad (r, s = 0, 1, \ldots) \tag{3.3}$$

i.e., the Hilbert matrix once more. Hence our general theory will yield the behavior of the smallest eigenvalue of the Nth section of the Hilbert matrix as a corollary [see Eq. (3.35)].

The central idea in the solution of the problem just stated is a simple one, namely that the question of the rate of approach of the $\{\lambda_N\}$ to 0 can be reduced to a question of the asymptotic rate of growth of a sequence of orthogonal polynomials. Since the latter problem has been extensively studied ([15], [39]) the former can be handled also. Let us sketch now the way in which this reduction comes about.

Let $w(x)$ be a weight function for the real interval $[a, b]$. Then under reasonable conditions there is a set $\{P_n(x)\}_{n=0}^{\infty}$ of orthogonal polynomials associated with $w(x)$. That is, $P_n(x)$ is of exact degree n, for each n, and

$$\int_a^b P_n(x) P_m(x) w(x) dx = \delta_{nm} \qquad (m, n = 0, 1, \ldots). \tag{3.4}$$

Suppose

$$P_n(x) = b_{n0} + b_{n1} x + \cdots + b_{nn} x^n \qquad (n = 0, 1, \ldots). \tag{3.5}$$

Then from (3.4),

$$\begin{aligned} \delta_{m,n} &= \sum_{i,j=0}^{N} b_{mi} b_{nj} \int_a^b x^{i+j} w(x) dx \\ &= \sum_{i,j=0}^{N} b_{mi} b_{mj} \mu_{i+j} \end{aligned} \tag{3.6}$$

where the μ_i are the moments of the weight function $w(x)$. Hence if we define

$$K_N = \begin{pmatrix} b_{00} & 0 & 0 & \ldots & 0 \\ b_{10} & b_{1,1} & 0 & \ldots & 0 \\ b_{2,0} & b_{2,1} & b_{2,2} & \ldots & 0 \\ \vdots & \vdots & \vdots & & \vdots \\ b_{N,0} & b_{N,1} & b_{N,2} & \ldots & b_{N,N} \end{pmatrix} \tag{3.7}$$

then, in matrix form, Eq. (3.6) becomes

$$I = K_N H_N K_N^T \tag{3.8}$$

where H_N is the Nth section of the Hankel matrix (μ_{i+j}). Hence (H_N is nonsingular and)

$$H_N^{-1} = K_N^T (K_N K_N^T) (K_N^T)^{-1}$$

so H_N^{-1} is similar to $K_N K_N^T$. But $K_N K_N^T$ has in its (m, n) entry

$$\begin{aligned}(K_N K_N^T)_{m,n} &= \sum_{i=0}^{N} b_{m,i} b_{n,i} \\ &= \frac{1}{2\pi} \int_0^{2\pi} P_m(e^{i\theta}) \overline{P_n(e^{i\theta})} d\theta \equiv a_{mn}\end{aligned} \tag{3.9}$$

and there follows

Lemma 1. *The inverse of the Nth section of the moments matrix (μ_{i+j}) is similar to a matrix whose m, n entry is given by a_{mn} of* (3.9), *where $\{P_n(x)\}$ are the associated orthogonal polynomials.*

To solve our problem concerning the rate of approach of λ_N to 0 we note that $1/\lambda_N$ is the largest eigenvalue of H_N^{-1}, and therefore is the largest eigenvalue of (3.9). From the well known asymptotic behavior of the $P_n(x)$, the behavior of the matrix entries for large m, n can be determined. It will turn out that the matrix (3.9) is asymptotically of rank 1 or 2, the eigenvalues of the rank 1 or 2 part can be explicitly found, and various estimates can be made to show that not much has been lost. We carry out this program in Section 3.3. These ideas and results are taken from Widom and Wilf [52].

In the next section we review the classical results on the growth of orthogonal polynomials which will be needed. Following the discussion of the lowest eigenvalue of H_N we turn to the largest eigenvalue, giving a theorem of Nehari which yields the precise conditions under which the spectra of the sections of Hankel matrices are uniformly bounded. We then discuss a theorem of Widom which settles a problem raised in the previous chapter on the spectral density of Hankel matrices in general, and the Hilbert matrix in particular. The chapter concludes with a survey of related results and generalizations.

3.2 Asymptotic Growth of Orthogonal Polynomials

If $w(x)$ is nonnegative on the real interval $[a, b]$, and if $w(x)$ stays away from zero in the sense that

$$\int_a^b ((\log w))/\sqrt{(x-a)(b-x)})dx > -\infty \tag{3.10}$$

then we give here the asymptotic behavior of the sequence of orthogonal polynomials $P_n(x)$ defined by

$$\int_a^b P_m(x) P_n(x) w(x) dx = \delta_{nm} \qquad (n, m = 0, 1, \ldots). \tag{3.11}$$

Similarly, if $f(\theta)$ is real valued, nonnegative and $\mathscr{L}(-\pi,\pi)$, and if

$$\int_{-\pi}^{\pi} f(\theta)d\theta > 0; \qquad \int_{-\pi}^{\pi} |\log f(\theta)|d\theta < \infty \tag{3.12}$$

we give the behavior of the sequence of polynomials $\{\phi_m(z)\}$ which are orthogonal on the unit circle in the sense that

$$\frac{1}{2\pi}\int_{-\pi}^{\pi} f(\theta)\phi_n(e^{i\theta})\overline{\phi_m(e^{i\theta})}\,d\theta = \delta_{nm} \qquad (n, m = 0, 1, 2, \ldots) \tag{3.13}$$

where $\phi_m(z)$ is a polynomial of exact degree m.

First, if $f(\theta)$ is a nonnegative trigonometric *polynomial, i.e.*, f has real coefficients and $f(\theta) \geqq 0$ for all real θ, then $f(\theta)$ can be represented as

$$f(\theta) = |h(z)|^2 \qquad (z = e^{i\theta}) \tag{3.14}$$

where $h(z)$ is a polynomial of the same degree as g. We can further suppose that in this representation $h(z) \neq 0$ for $|z| < 1$, and $h(0) > 0$. Then the polynomial $h(z)$ is uniquely determined. This theorem is due to Fejér, and a proof is in [32].

Now suppose $f(\theta)$, no longer necessarily a polynomial, is nonnegative and satisfies (3.12). We ask if $f(\theta)$ is still representable as the squared modulus of the boundary values of some function regular in the circle. The answer is that this is so, and we can write

$$f(\theta) = |D(e^{i\theta})|^2 \tag{3.15}$$

where $D(z)$ is regular and bounded in $|z| < 1$, has radial limits for almost all θ on the circle, has no zeros in $|z| < 1$, and is real and positive at the origin. This function is not uniquely determined by these conditions, but one such can be found as follows (all missing proofs are in [39]):

Define a harmonic function by the Poisson integral formula applied to the boundary values $1/2 \log f(\theta)$, namely

$$u(re^{i\theta}) = \frac{1}{2\pi}\int_{-\pi}^{\pi}\left(\frac{1}{2}\log f(t)\right)\frac{1-r^2}{1-2r\cos(\theta-t)+r^2}\,dt \qquad (0 \leqq r < 1). \tag{3.16}$$

We then take $D(z) = e^{u(z)+iv(z)}$ where $v(z)$ is the conjugate harmonic function which vanishes at the origin. It can be shown that

$$\lim_{r\to 1^-} u(re^{i\theta}) = 1/2 \log f(\theta)$$

for almost all θ, and this implies that

$$\lim_{r\to 1^-} D(re^{i\theta}) \equiv D(e^{i\theta})$$

exists for almost all θ, that

$$|D(e^{i\theta})|^2 = \{e^{1/2 \log f(\theta)}\}^2 = f(\theta)$$

and so that $D(z)$ provides the required representation.

Explicitly,

$$D(z) = \exp\left\{\frac{1}{4\pi}\int_{-\pi}^{\pi} \log f(t)\frac{1+ze^{it}}{1-ze^{-it}}\,dt\right\} \quad (|z|<1). \tag{3.17}$$

The connection between this $D(z)$ and the asymptotic expansions is easy to see in one special case, namely where the weight function for a system of polynomials orthogonal in the unit circle is

$$f(\theta) = 1/g(\theta) \tag{3.18}$$

where $g(\theta)$ is a positive trigonometric polynomial. For in that case, the system of polynomials $\{\phi_n(z)\}$ is explicitly given by

$$\begin{aligned}\phi_n(z) &= z^{n-m}\overline{D(z)}\\ &= z^n\bar{D}(1/z)\end{aligned} \tag{3.19}$$

for $n \geqq m$, where m is the degree of g and $D(z)$ is the (polynomial) representation of g as a square. (3.19) can be checked by choosing any polynomial $q(z)$ of degree $n-1$, and then

$$\begin{aligned}\frac{1}{2\pi}\int_{-\pi}^{\pi} f(\theta)\phi_n(e^{i\theta})q(e^{i\theta})d\theta &= \frac{1}{2\pi}\int_{|z|=1}\left\{D(z)\bar{D}\left(\frac{1}{z}\right)\right\}^{-1}\left\{z^n\left(\bar{D}\left(\frac{1}{z}\right)\right)\right\}\bar{q}\left(\frac{1}{z}\right)\frac{dz}{iz}\\ &= \frac{1}{2\pi i}\int_{|z|=1}\left(z^{n-1}\bar{q}\left(\frac{1}{z}\right)/D(z)\right)dz = 0\end{aligned}$$

by Cauchy's theorem.

Hence, for polynomials orthogonal on the unit circle with a weight function of the form (3.18) the asymptotic behavior coincides with an explicit formula, namely (3.19), for the polynomials themselves.

More generally, for the sequence $\{\phi_n(z)\}$ associated with an arbitrary $f(\theta)$, subject only to (3.12) we have

$$\phi_n(z) \sim z^n\{\bar{D}(1/z)\}^{-1} \qquad (n\to\infty) \tag{3.20}$$

uniformly for $|z| \geqq 1+\delta$, where $D(z)$ corresponds to $f(\theta)$ as in (3.15), or more explicitly, (3.17).

Since the mapping $x=(1/2)(z+1/z)$ carries the exterior of the unit disc in the z plane into the exterior of the interval $[-1,1]$, we have for polynomials orthogonal on $[-1,1]$ the estimate

$$\phi_n(z) \sim (1/\sqrt{2\pi})\, z^n \{D(1/z)\}^{-1}$$

uniformly for x bounded away from the interval, where $D(z)$ corresponds to the weight function

$$f(\theta) = w(\cos\theta)\,|\sin\theta|$$

on the circle, and $w(x)$ is the given weight function on $[-1,1]$. Finally, after a change of scale and translation, we obtain the following result on an arbitrary real interval $[a,b]$.

Theorem 3.1. *Let $w(x)$ be a weight function, satisfying* (3.10), *on the interval $[a,b]$. Let $\{\phi_n(x)\}$ be the orthogonal sequence of polynomials corresponding to $w(x)$. Then, uniformly for z bounded away from $[a,b]$ we have*

$$\phi_n(z) \sim (1/\sqrt{\pi(b-a)})\, \zeta^n A(\zeta) \qquad (n\to\infty) \tag{3.21}$$

where

$$\zeta = \frac{2}{b-a} z - \frac{a+b}{b-a} + \left[\left(\frac{2}{b-a} z - \frac{b+a}{b-a}\right)^2 - 1\right]^{1/2} \tag{3.22}$$

$$\log|A(\varrho e^{i\phi})| \tag{3.23}$$

$$= \frac{-1}{4\pi} \int_{-\pi}^{\pi} \log\left[w\left(\frac{b-a}{2}\cos t + \frac{b+a}{2}\right)|\sin t|\right] \frac{\varrho^2-1}{1-2\varrho\cos(\phi-t)+\varrho^2}\, dt$$

and the square root in (3.22) *is the branch which is positive for $z\to+\infty$.*

3.3 The Lowest Eigenvalue of Sections of a Moments Matrix

Now we suppose that a weight function satisfying (3.10) is given, and that its moments are

$$C_m = \int_a^b x^m w(x)\,dx \qquad (m=0,1,2,\ldots). \tag{3.24}$$

We let

$$H_N = (C_{m+n}) \qquad (0 \leqq m, n \leqq N)$$

and let λ_N be the smallest eigenvalue of H_N. We seek the asymptotic behavior of λ_N for $N \to \infty$.

In Theorem 3.1 the dominant element is the factor ζ^n, so the first question concerns the maximum of $|\zeta| = |\zeta(z)|$ as z runs over $|z|=1$, where $\zeta(z)$ is given by (3.22). Simply by differentiating $|\zeta(e^{i\theta})|^2$ one finds that $\max_\theta |\zeta(e^{i\theta})| = \sigma$ where

$$\sigma = \begin{cases} \dfrac{b+a+2}{b-a} + \left[\left(\dfrac{b+a+2}{b-a}\right)^2 - 1\right]^{1/2} & \text{(Cases 1 and 2)} \\ \left(\dfrac{1}{b|a|} + 1\right)^{1/2} + \left(\dfrac{1}{|a|b}\right)^{1/2} & \text{(Cases 2 and 3)} \end{cases} \tag{3.25}$$

and the cases are distinguished by

Case 1: $a > -b(1+2b)^{-1}$,

Case 2: $a = -b(1+2b)^{-1}$,

Case 3: $a < -b(1+2b)^{-1}$.

We always assume that $a+b \geqq 0$, which can be done without loss of generality. It is furthermore true that in cases 1 and 2 the maximum σ occurs only at $\theta = \pi$, while in case 3 it occurs only at $\theta = \pm\theta_0$ where

$$\cos\theta_0 = (a+b)/2ab\,. \tag{3.26}$$

In Cases 1 and 3 $g'' \neq 0$ at the maximum, while in Case 2 $g'' = 0$ but $g^{(iv)} \neq 0$, where

$$g(\theta) = |\zeta(e^{i\theta})|\,. \tag{3.27}$$

Lemma 1. *If a_{mn} are defined by* (3.9) *then*

$$|a_{mn}| \leqq \begin{cases} A\sigma^{m+n}/\sqrt{m+n+1} & \textit{Cases 1 and 3} \\ A\sigma^{m+n}/(m+n+1)^{1/4} & \textit{Case 2}\,. \end{cases} \tag{3.28}$$

Proof. Suppose the unit circle does not intersect the interval $[a,b]$. Then

$$\begin{aligned} |a_{mn}| &= \left|(1/2\pi)\int_0^{2\pi} P_m(e^{i\theta})\overline{P_n(e^{i\theta})}\,d\theta\right| \\ &\leqq A\int_0^{2\pi} g(\theta)^{m+n}\,d\theta\,. \end{aligned}$$

By the well known Laplace expansion for integrals [9] the last is

$$O(\sigma^{m+n}/\sqrt{m+n+1})$$

if the maximum is of second order (Cases 1 and 3), and

$$O(\sigma^{m+n}/(m+n+1)^{1/4})$$

for the fourth order maximum of Case 2.

Otherwise, suppose $1 \in [a, b]$, $-1 \notin [a, b]$. Then choose $\varepsilon > 0$ and we have

$$
\begin{aligned}
|a_{mn}| &\leqq (1/2\pi) \int_{-\varepsilon}^{\varepsilon} |P_m(e^{i\theta}) P_n(e^{i\theta})| d\theta \\
&\quad + (1/2\pi) \int_{\varepsilon}^{2\pi-\varepsilon} |P_m(e^{i\theta}) P_n(e^{i\theta})| d\theta \\
&\equiv I_1 + I_2
\end{aligned}
$$

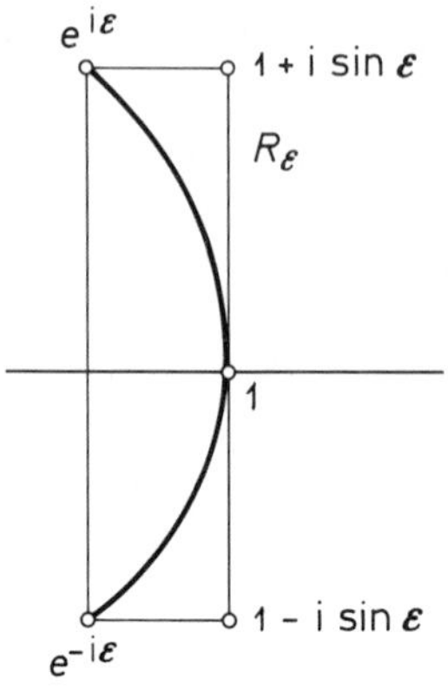

say. Now in I_2 the arguments of the polynomials are bounded away from $[a, b]$, the uniform estimates of Theorem 3.1 hold, and we obtain an estimate of the desired form. For I_1, consider the rectangle R_ε whose vertices are $e^{\pm i\varepsilon}$, $1 \pm i \sin \varepsilon$. It contains in its interior the arc $|\theta| \leqq \varepsilon$ of the unit circle. Since the orthogonal polynomials have only real zeros, each factor of $P_n(z)$, and so $P_n(z)$ itself, assumes its maximum modulus in R_ε on the horizontal sides of R_ε, and the same is true of $P_m(z) P_n(z)$. On these sides we have again the estimate of Theorem 3.1 and we obtain

$$
\limsup_{m+n \to \infty} \max_{z \in R_\varepsilon} |P_m(z) P_n(z)|^{1/m+n} = g(\varepsilon + O(\varepsilon^2)).
$$

Hence for $m+n \to \infty$, $I_1 = O(t^{m+n})$ for any $t > g(\varepsilon + O(\varepsilon^2))$. But $g(2\varepsilon)$ is such a t and so $I_1 = O(g(2\varepsilon)^{m+n})$. For ε small enough, however, $g(2\varepsilon) < \sigma$ because $g(\theta)$ does not assume its maximum at $\theta = 0$, whence

$$
I_1 = O(\sigma^{m+n} / \sqrt{m+n}), \qquad m+n \to \infty
$$

proving the lemma.

Now suppose that the unit circle does not intersect the interval $[a, b]$. Then

$$
\begin{aligned}
a_{mn} &= (1/2\pi) \int_{-\pi}^{\pi} P_m(e^{i\theta}) \overline{P_n(e^{i\theta})} d\theta \\
&= (1/2\pi) \int_{-\pi}^{\pi} \left\{ \frac{\zeta^m A(\zeta)}{\sqrt{\pi(b-a)}} \, \frac{\zeta^{-n} \overline{A(\zeta)}}{\sqrt{\pi(b-a)}} \right\} d\theta \qquad (\zeta = e^{i\theta}) \\
&= \frac{1}{2\pi^2(b-a)} \int_{-\pi}^{\pi} \{ g(\theta)^{m+n} [\operatorname{sgn} \zeta(e^{i\theta})]^{m-n} A(\zeta(e^{i\theta}))|^2 + o(g(\theta)^{m+n}) \} d\theta
\end{aligned}
$$

where $\operatorname{sgn} z = e^{i\alpha}$ if $z = |z| e^{i\alpha}$. It is now easy to determine the asymptotic behavior of the matrix elements a_{mn} as $m, n \to \infty$ with $m-n$ remaining bounded. In case 1, for example, the maximum of $g(\theta)$ occurs only at $\theta = \pi$, and by the Laplace method for asymptotic expansion of an integral

$$\begin{aligned} a_{mn} &\sim \gamma(-1)^{m+n}(\sigma^{m+n}/\sqrt{m+n}) \\ \gamma &= |A(\zeta(-1))|^2 \sigma^{1/2}/2^{1/2}\pi^{3/2}(b-a)\sqrt{g''(\pi)}\,. \end{aligned} \tag{3.29}$$

In case 2,

$$\begin{aligned} a_{mn} &\sim \gamma(-1)^{m-n}(\sigma^{m+n}/(m+n)^{1/4}), \\ \gamma &= \frac{3^{1/4}\Gamma(1/4)|A(\zeta(-1))|^2\sigma^{1/4}}{2^{9/4}\pi^2|g^{(iv)}(\pi)|^{1/4}(b-a)} \end{aligned} \tag{3.30}$$

while in Case 3,

$$\begin{aligned} a_{mn} &= \frac{\gamma\cos[(m-n)\phi_0]\sigma^{m+n}}{\sqrt{m+n}} + o\left(\frac{\sigma^{m+n}}{\sqrt{m+n}}\right)(e^{i\phi_0} = \operatorname{sgn}\zeta(e^{i\theta_0})), \\ \gamma &= \frac{\sqrt{2\sigma}|A(\zeta(e^{i\theta_0}))|^2}{\pi^{3/2}|g''(\theta_0)|^{1/2}(b-a)}\,. \end{aligned} \tag{3.31}$$

If the unit circle intersects $[a, b]$ we treat the matter as in the lemma, obtaining the same results.

We will now find the behavior of the eigenvalue λ_N. In case 1, put

$$b_{mn} = (-1)^{m+n}\sigma^{m+n}$$

and

$$c_{mn} = a_{mn} - (\gamma/\sqrt{2N})\, b_{mn}\,.$$

With an N_0 and an ε fixed, (3.29) implies that for m, n large enough, $|m-n| \leqq N_0$

$$|a_{mn} - \gamma(-1)^{m+n}(\sigma^{m+n}/\sqrt{m+n})| \leqq \varepsilon(\sigma^{m+n}/\sqrt{m+n})\,.$$

Thus if N is large enough, $m \geqq N - N_0$, $n \geqq N - N_0$,

$$\begin{aligned} |c_{mn}| &= |a_{mn} - (\gamma/\sqrt{2N})(-1)^{m-n}\sigma^{m+n}| \\ &\leqq |a_{mn} - \gamma(-1)^{m+n}(\sigma^{m+n}/\sqrt{m+n})| + |\gamma\sigma^{m+n}[1/\sqrt{2N} - 1/\sqrt{m+n}] \\ &\leqq \varepsilon/\sqrt{N})\,\sigma^{m+n}\,. \end{aligned}$$

However, from Lemma 1,

$$|c_{mn}| \leqq K A \sigma^{m+n}/\sqrt{m+n+1} \tag{3.32}$$

for all m, n.

Let μ_N be the eigenvalue of maximum modulus of $(c_{mn})_{m,n=0}^{N}$. Then

$$\begin{aligned}\mu_N^2 &\leqq \sum_{m,n=0}^{N} c_{mn}^2\\ &\leqq \frac{\varepsilon^2}{N}\sum_{m,n=N-N_0}^{N}\sigma^{2(m+n)}+K\sum_{m=0}^{N-N_0}\sum_{n=0}^{N}\frac{\sigma^{2(m+n)}}{m+n+1}\\ &\leqq \varepsilon^2\sigma^{4N+4}/N(\sigma^2-1)^2+K\left(\sigma^{2(2N-N_0)}/(2N-N_0)\right).\end{aligned}$$

Hence for N_0 large enough, and N large enough in comparison to N_0,

$$|\mu_N|\leqq 2\varepsilon\sigma^{2(N+1)}/(\sigma^2-1)\sqrt{N}. \tag{3.33}$$

Now λ_N^{-1} is the largest eigenvalue of $(a_{m,n})$, μ_N the largest of (c_{mn}), and let v_N be the largest of $(b_{m,n})_{m,n=0}^{N}$. Then

$$\gamma v_N/\sqrt{2N}-\mu_N\leqq\lambda_N^{-1}\leqq\gamma v_N/\sqrt{2N}+\mu_N$$

and so

$$\frac{\gamma v_N}{\sqrt{2N}}-\frac{2\varepsilon\sigma^{2N+2}}{(\sigma^2-1)\sqrt{N}}\leqq\lambda_N^{-1}\leqq\frac{\gamma v_N}{\sqrt{2N}}+\frac{2\varepsilon\sigma^{2N+2}}{(\sigma^2-1)\sqrt{N}}.$$

But $(b_{mn})_0^N$ is of rank 1, so its largest (and only nonzero) eigenvalue is

$$v_N=\sum_{m=0}^{N}\sigma^{2m}=(\sigma^{2(N+1)}-1)/(\sigma^2-1).$$

Hence

$$\begin{aligned}\lambda_N&\sim\sqrt{2N}/\gamma v_N\\ &\sim(\sigma^2-1)\sqrt{2N}/\gamma\sigma^{2N+2}\qquad(N\to\infty)\end{aligned}$$

in Case 1. Case 2 is handled the same way, as is Case 3, where the only complication is that the matrix

$$(b_{mn})_{m,n=0}^{N}$$

turns out to be of rank 2 instead of rank 1, in fact

$$\begin{aligned}b_{mn}&=\cos\left[(m-n)\phi_0\right]\sigma^{m+n}+(\sigma^{m+n})\\ &=\{(\cos m\phi_0)\sigma^m\}\{(\cos n\phi_0)\sigma^n\}+\{(\sin m\phi_0)\sigma^m\}\{(\sin n\phi_0)\sigma^n\}\end{aligned}$$

whereas it is clear that the only nonzero eigenvalues of

$$u_m u_n+v_m v_n\qquad(m,n=0,1,\ldots,N)$$

are the two eigenvalues of the 2×2-matrix

$$\begin{pmatrix}(u,u) & (u,v)\\ (u,v) & (v,v)\end{pmatrix}$$

and that leads easily to the result stated below (Widom and Wilf [52]).

Theorem 3.2. *Let λ_N be the lowest eigenvalue of the Nth section of the moments matrix of a weight function $w(x)$ satisfying* (3.10). *Then*

$$\begin{aligned}
&\text{(a)}\ \lambda_N \sim (\sqrt{2N}/\gamma)(\sigma^2-1)\sigma^{-2N-2} \qquad \textit{(Case 1)},\\
&\text{(b)}\ \lambda_N \sim ((2N)^{1/4}/\gamma)(\sigma^2-1)\sigma^{-2N-2} \qquad \textit{(Case 2)},\\
&\text{(c)}\ \lambda_N \sim \frac{2\sqrt{2N}}{\gamma}\left[\frac{1}{\sigma^2-1}+\left(\frac{1}{\sigma^4-2\sigma^2\cos 2\phi_0-1}\right)^{1/2}\right]^{-1}\sigma^{-2N-2}\\
&\textit{(Case 3)}\,.
\end{aligned} \tag{3.34}$$

The Hilbert matrix

$$(1/(m+n+1))_{m,n=0}^{N}$$

arises from the moments matrix of $w(x)\equiv 1$ on $[a,b]=[0,1]$. Then we are in Case 1, and (3.25) gives $\sigma=+2\sqrt{2}$, while from (3.22), (3.23),

$$\zeta = 2z-1+2[z^2-z]^{1/2}$$

and

$$\log|A(\varrho e^{i\phi})| = \frac{-1}{4\pi}\int_{-\pi}^{\pi}(\log|\sin t|)\frac{\varrho^2-1}{1-2\varrho\cos(\phi-t)+\varrho^2}\,dt\,.$$

After some calculation we find that the lowest eigenvalue of the Hilbert matrix $(1/(m+n+1))_{m,n=0}^{N}$ is

$$\lambda_N \sim \pi^{3/2}(8+6\sqrt{2})^{5/2}\sqrt{N}(1+\sqrt{2})^{-4N-9} \qquad (N\to\infty)\,. \tag{3.35}$$

This result is clearly equivalent to a theorem about polynomial approximation to zero: Among all polynomials f of degree N such that

$$(1/2\pi)\int_0^{2\pi}|f(e^{i\theta})|^2\,d\theta = 1 \tag{3.36}$$

the minimum value of

$$\int_0^1 |f(x)|^2\,dx$$

is the λ_N of (3.35). In general, the eigenvalue λ_N for a weight function $w(x)$ is the minimum of

$$\int_a^b |f(x)|^2 w(x)\,dx$$

in the class of polynomials of degree N, normalized by (3.36).

3.4 Generalizations

It is tempting to visualize a unified theory in which Hankel and Toeplitz forms would both appear as special cases. Such a theory would begin with a measure μ supported on a set E in the complex plane and the moments

$$C_{m,n} = \int_E z^m \bar{z}^n d\mu(z) . \qquad (3.37)$$

If E is the unit circle, $C_{m,n} = C_{m-n}$ and we have the Toeplitz theory, whereas if E is a real interval $C_{m,n} = C_{m+n}$ and we have Hankel forms. It appears to be a question of some difficulty, however, to deduce growth theorems for the orthogonal polynomials associated with μ of sufficient precision to reproduce the known results for both Hankel and Toeplitz forms.

If E is a union of a finite collection of Jordan arcs and regions bounded by Jordan curves then the relation

$$\lim_{n\to\infty} \max_{z\in E} |P_n(z)|^{1/n} = C(E) \qquad (3.38)$$

was proved by Geronimus [14], where $C(E)$ is the capacity of E, and $P_n(z)$ is the associated system of orthogonal polynomials, under certain restrictions on μ. This was generalized by Widom [50] to arbitrary compact sets, under certain restrictions on μ, and it was then shown, by the methods of section 3.3, that the sequence $\lambda_N^{1/N}$ approaches a limit, where λ_N is the lowest eigenvalue of the Nth section of (3.37). In [45] Widom refined these estimates to obtain the growth of λ_N itself, for systems of Jordan curves or systems of Jordan arcs and curves. He showed there that

$$\lambda_N \sim (\pi/\Gamma(1/m+1)) K_N(s_0, s_0)^{-1} (2u_0 N)^{1/m} e^{-2\tau N} \qquad (N\to\infty) \quad (3.39)$$

where K_N is the Szegö kernel function, and u_0, s_0, m, τ are certain parameters which are determined by the maximum value of a function $g(s)$ defined by an extremum problem associated with the measure. Eq. (3.39) holds if the maximum value is assumed only once, with a slightly more complicated result holding for higher multiplicities.

For measures carried on noncompact support little is known. In special cases where asymptotic formulas for orthogonal polynomials are available, asymptotic information about λ_N follows readily. Thus, for the Laguerre polynomials, associated with e^{-x} on $[0, \infty)$ we have

$$L_n(x) = (1/2\sqrt{\pi}) e^{x/2} (-nx)^{-1/4} e^{2\sqrt{-nx}} \{1 + O(n^{-1/2})\} \qquad (n\to\infty) \quad (3.40)$$

uniformly for x bounded away from the positive real axis. Then it is not hard to show that for the lowest eigenvalue λ_N of the matrix

$$(m+n)! \qquad (m, n=0, 1, \ldots, N) \tag{3.41}$$

we have

$$\lambda_N \sim 16\pi^2 e N^{1/4} e^{-4\sqrt{N}} \qquad (N \to \infty). \tag{3.42}$$

General results of this kind will have to await the development of growth theorems for orthogonal polynomials on unbounded systems of curves.

3.5 Upper Bounds

In the case of Hankel matrices the theory of the largest eigenvalue of the nth section is in a very primitive condition. Not only are there no general theorems for the rate of approach to the uniform upper bound, but only fairly recently has a criterion been given for determining whether or not the sections are uniformly bounded, and if so, finding the bound. This theory is due to Nehari [27]. A shorter proof has been found by Wang [44]. It identifies the sequences $\{\alpha(m)\}_0^\infty$ for which the matrices $\alpha(\mu+\nu)_0^N$ are uniformly bounded as the Fourier coefficients of bounded functions. Indeed, if

$$\alpha(n) = (1/2\pi) \int_0^{2\pi} F(\theta) e^{-in\theta} d\theta \qquad (n=0, 1, 2, \ldots) \tag{3.43}$$

where

$$\operatorname*{ess\,sup}_{\theta} |F(\theta)| = M \tag{3.44}$$

then, if $\sum |x_\nu|^2 < \infty$ we have for $\varrho < 1$

$$\begin{aligned}
\left|\sum_{\mu,\nu=0}^{\infty} \alpha(\mu+\nu)\varrho^{\mu+\nu} x_\mu x_\nu\right| &= \left|\sum_{\mu,\nu=0}^{\infty} x_\mu x_\nu \varrho^{\mu+\nu} \frac{1}{2\pi}\int_0^{2\pi} F(\theta) e^{-i(\mu+\nu)\theta} d\theta\right| \\
&= (1/2\pi)\left|\int_0^{2\pi} F(\theta)\left(\sum_{\nu=0}^{\infty} x_\nu \varrho^\nu e^{-i\nu\theta}\right)^2 d\theta\right| \\
&\leqq (M/2\pi)\int_0^{2\pi} \left|\sum x_\nu \varrho^\nu e^{-i\nu\theta}\right|^2 d\theta \\
&= M \sum |x_\nu|^2 \varrho^{2\nu} \\
&\leqq M \sum |x_\nu|^2
\end{aligned}$$

and if we let $\varrho \to 1$ we obtain the bound M for the matrix $\alpha(\mu+\nu)]_0^\infty$. Conversely, we have to show that if the matrix is bounded by M then there is an F of the type (3.43), (3.44).

Lemma 1. *Let $P(z)$ be a given polynomial of degree n. Then there are constants $\lambda, t, \beta_1, \ldots, \beta_n$ with $\lambda > 0, 0 \leqq t \leqq \pi, |\beta_\nu| < 1$ such that*

$$\lambda e^{2it} \prod_{\nu=1}^{n} (\beta_\nu + z)/(1 + \overline{\beta}_\nu z) = P(z) + z^n q(z) \tag{3.45}$$

where $q(0) = 0$ and q is analytic in $|z| < 1$.

Proof. For a given function ϕ, regular in $|z| < 1$, consider the maximum $\lambda = \lambda(\phi)$ of $|P(z) + z^{n+1}\phi(z)|$ for $|z| < 1$, and the problem of minimizing $\lambda(\phi)$ by choice of ϕ. We solve this by an algorithm of Schur [35], which was devised by him for the purpose of giving a test, on the coefficients of an analytic function, to determine whether or not the function is is bounded in the unit disc. Write

$$g_0(z) = \lambda^{-1}(P(z) + z^{n+1}\phi(z))$$

and recursively define

$$g_{\mu+1}(z) = (g_\mu(z) - g_\mu(0))/z\{1 - \overline{g_\mu(0)} g_\mu(z)\} \quad (\mu = 0, 1, \ldots, n). \tag{3.46}$$

Then $|g_0(z)| \leqq 1$ $(|z| < 1)$ implies $|g_\mu(z)| \leqq 1$ ($|z| < 1$ for $\mu = 0, 1, \ldots, n+1$. Further, if $|g_{n+1}(0)| = 1$, then $|g_{n+1}(z)| \equiv 1$, and applying (3.46) backwards, starting from $g_{n+1}(z) = ze^{i\xi}$, we obtain the left side of (3.45) for $\lambda g_0(z)$. Otherwise, $|g_{n+1}(0)| < 1$, and if we start with $g_{n+1}(z) \equiv g_{n+1}(0)$, and work backwards to $g_0(z)$ by (3.46) then we find that

$$g_0(z) = \lambda^{-1} P(z) + O(z^{n+1})$$

and $|g_0(z)| \leqq 1 - \varepsilon$ for $|z| < 1$. Hence

$$\lambda |g_0(z)| = |P(z) + O(z^{n+1})| \leqq \lambda(1 - \varepsilon)$$

and therefore $\lambda g_0(z)$ cannot give a minimum to the functional $\lambda(\phi)$ unless $\lambda g_0(z)$ is of the form shown on the left side of (3.45). But there is an attained minimum for $\lambda(\phi)$, hence there is a function satisfying (3.45), and so the lemma is proved.

Lemma 2. *If $P(z)$ is a given polynomial of degree n, then there exist functions $g(z), h(z)$ such that g, h are regular in $|z| \leqq 1, g(0) = 0$, and for $|z| = 1$ we have*

$$(\overline{P(z)} + g(z))h(z) = \lambda \overline{h(z)}. \tag{3.47}$$

Proof. Suppose $P(z) = \sum_0^n \gamma_\nu z^\nu$, $\overline{P}(z) = \sum_0^n \overline{\gamma}_\nu z^\nu$. Let $g(z), \lambda, t, \beta_1, \ldots, \beta_n$ be determined by Lemma 1 applied to $\overline{P}(z)$, and define

$$h(z) = e^{-it} \prod_{\nu=1}^{n} (1 + \overline{\beta}_\nu z).$$

Then

$$\begin{aligned}(\overline{P(z)}+g(z))h(z) &= (\bar{P}(\bar{z})+g(z))h(z)\\ &= \left(\sum_{\nu=0}^{n} \bar{\gamma}_\nu \bar{z}^\nu + g(z)\right) h(z)\\ &= z^{-n}\left(\sum_{\nu=0}^{n} \overline{\gamma_{n-\nu}} z^\nu + z^n g(z)\right) h(z)\\ &= z^{-n}(\bar{P}(z)+z^n g(z))h(z)\\ &= \lambda e^{it} z^{-n} \prod_{\nu=1}^{n} ((z+\beta_\nu)/(1+\bar{\beta}_\nu z)) \prod_{\nu=1}^{n} (1+\bar{\beta}_\nu z)\\ &= \lambda e^{it} z^{-n} \prod_{\nu=1}^{n} (\beta_\nu + z)\\ &= \lambda \overline{[e^{-it} \prod_{\nu=1}^{n} (1+\bar{\beta}_\nu z)]}\\ &= \lambda \overline{h(z)}\end{aligned}$$

as required.

Lemma 3. *Let* $\alpha(m)=0$ *for* $m=n+1, n+2, \ldots$. *If the Hankel matrix* $(a(\mu+\nu))_0^\infty$ *is bounded by* M *then there is a function* $F \in L^2(0, 2\pi)$ *such that* (3.43), (3.44) *hold.*

Proof. Write

$$P(z) = \sum_{m=0}^{n} \overline{\alpha(m)} z^m$$

and let $g(z)$, $h(z)$ be determined by Lemma 2. We claim that

$$F(\theta) = \overline{P(e^{i\theta})} + g(e^{i\theta})$$

has the desired properties. Then, if $g(z) = \sum_1^\infty c_\nu z^\nu$, we have

$$\begin{aligned}\sum_{\mu,\nu} \alpha(\mu+\nu) x_\mu x_\nu &= \frac{1}{2\pi}\int_0^{2\pi} \left(\sum_{\nu=0}^{n} \alpha(\nu) e^{-i\nu\theta} + \sum_{\nu=1}^{\infty} c_\nu e^{i\nu\theta}\right)\left(\sum_{\nu=0}^{\infty} x_\nu e^{i\nu\theta}\right)^2 d\theta \\ &= \frac{1}{2\pi}\int_0^{2\pi} (\overline{P(e^{i\theta})} + g(e^{i\theta})) h^2(e^{i\theta}) d\theta\,.\end{aligned} \tag{3.48}$$

But (3.47) implies two things, namely

$$|\overline{P(z)} + q(z)| \equiv \lambda \qquad (|z|=1)$$

and

$$(\overline{P(z)} + q(z)) h^2(z) > 0 \qquad (|z|=1)\,.$$

Thus the right side of (3.48) is

$$(\lambda/\pi)\int_0^{2\pi}|h(e^{i\theta})|^2\,d\theta$$

and so, since the form is bounded by M,

$$(\lambda/2\pi)\int_0^{2\pi}|h(e^{i\theta})|^2\,d\theta \leqq M\sum x_\mu^2$$
$$=(M/2\pi)\int_0^{2\pi}|h(e^{i\theta})|^2\,d\theta\,.$$

It follows that $\lambda\leqq M$, and therefore that $|F(\theta)|\equiv M$, proving the lemma. Next we partially relax the hypothesis that only finitely many $\alpha(\nu)$ are nonzero.

Lemma 4. *Let*

$$P(z)=\sum_{m=0}^{\infty}\overline{\alpha(m)}\,z^m$$

and suppose $P(z)$ is regular in $|z|\leqq 1$. If the Hankel matrix $(\alpha(\mu+\nu))_0^\infty$ is bounded by M, then there is a function $F\in\mathscr{L}^2(0,2\pi)$ such that (3.43), (3.44) *hold.*

Proof. Given $\varepsilon>0$, find a polynomial $P_n(z)$ such that

$$|P(z)-P_n(z)|\leqq\varepsilon\qquad(|z|\leqq 1)\,.$$

Choose an l^2 sequence $x_0, x_1, x_2, \ldots$. Then, if $h(z)=\sum_0^\infty x_\mu z^\mu$,

$$\sum_{\mu,\nu=0}^{\infty}\alpha(\mu+\nu)x_\mu x_\nu=(1/2\pi)\int_0^{2\pi}\overline{P_n(e^{i\theta})}\,h^2(e^{i\theta})\,d\theta$$
$$+(1/2\pi)\int_0^{2\pi}\overline{[P(\theta)-P_n(e^{i\theta})]}\,h^2(e^{i\theta})\,d\theta$$

whence

$$\left|\frac{1}{2\pi}\int_0^{2\pi}\overline{P_n(e^{i\theta})}\,h^2(e^{i\theta})\,d\theta\right|\leqq M\sum|x_\mu|^2+\varepsilon\sum|x_\mu|^2$$
$$=(M+\varepsilon)\sum x_\mu^2\,.$$

Apply Lemma 2 to $P_n(z)$. Then there is a $g_n(z)$, with $g_n(0)=0$, such that $|\overline{P_n(e^{i\theta})}+g_n(e^{i\theta})|=\lambda\leqq M+\varepsilon$. Hence

$$|\overline{P(e^{i\theta})}+g_n(e^{i\theta})|\leqq M+2\varepsilon\,.$$

Since $g_n(0)=0$,

$$\int_0^{2\pi} P_n(e^{i\theta})g_n(e^{i\theta})d\theta=0$$

and we have, for $0<\varrho<1$,

$$\begin{aligned}\frac{1}{2\pi}\int_0^{2\pi}|g_n(\varrho e^{i\theta})|^2 d\theta &\leqq \frac{1}{2\pi}\int_0^{2\pi}|g_n(e^{i\theta})|^2 d\theta\\ &\leqq \frac{1}{2\pi}\int_0^{2\pi}|P_n(e^{i\theta})|^2 d\theta+\frac{1}{2\pi}\int_0^{2\pi}|g_n(e^{i\theta})|^2 d\theta\\ &=\frac{1}{2\pi}\int_0^{2\pi}|\overline{P_n(e^{i\theta})}+g_n(e^{i\theta})|^2 d\theta\\ &\leqq (M+\varepsilon)^2 .\end{aligned}$$

Choose a sequence $\varepsilon_0\geqq\varepsilon_1\geqq\varepsilon_2\geqq\cdots$ of $\varepsilon_j\to 0$. Then for each n, find a g_n such that

$$\frac{1}{2\pi}\int_0^{2\pi}|g_n(\varrho e^{i\theta})|^2 d\theta\leqq(M+\varepsilon_n)^2\leqq(M+\varepsilon_0)^2 . \tag{3.49}$$

All of these g_n lie in the set of functions determined by the outermost inequality in (3.49). This is a compact set, so the $g_n\to g$ uniformly on a subsequence of n. Evidently

$$|\overline{P(z)}+g_n(z)|\leqq M+\varepsilon$$

for $|z|\leqq 1$ by the maximum principle, and letting $n\to\infty$

$$|\overline{P(z)}+g(z)|\leqq M \qquad (|z|<1) . \tag{3.50}$$

Further, by Fatou's lemma, for almost all θ the radial limit

$$\lim_{\varrho\to 1-0} g(\varrho e^{i\theta})=g(e^{i\theta})$$

exists, and so we have (3.50) for $|z|=1$ also.

If we put $F(\theta)=\overline{P(e^{i\theta})}+g(e^{i\theta})$, then $|F(\theta)|\leqq M$ almost everywhere and

$$\begin{aligned}\frac{1}{2\pi}\int_0^{2\pi}F(\theta)e^{in\theta}d\theta &=\alpha(n)+\lim_{\varrho\to 1^-}\frac{1}{2\pi}\int_0^{2\pi}g(\varrho e^{i\theta})e^{in\theta}d\theta\\ &=\alpha(n)\end{aligned}$$

completing the proof of the lemma.

Lemma 5. *The conclusion of Lemma 4 remains true if $P(z)$ is regular only for $|z|<1$.*

Proof. Since the form is bounded by M, we have, if $0<\varrho<1$,

$$\left|\sum_{\mu,\nu=0}^{\infty} \alpha(\mu+\nu)\varrho^{\mu+\nu} x_\mu x_\nu\right| \leqq M \sum_{\mu=0}^{\infty} |x_\mu|^2 .$$

The sequence $\{\varrho^\mu \alpha(\mu)\}$ satisfies the stronger hypothesis of Lemma 4, and a compactness argument yields the result.

It remains only to show that the conclusion holds for sequences $\{\alpha(\nu)\}$ such that $P(z)$ is not regular in $|z|<1$. There are none of these, however, for if the form $\alpha(\mu+\nu)]_0^\infty$ is bounded by M, then $\{\alpha_\nu\}_0^\infty$ is l^2. Indeed, the bilinear form

$$B = \sum_{\mu,\nu=0}^{\infty} \alpha(\mu+\nu) a_\mu b_\nu$$

is bounded by $M\|a\|\;\|b\|$. Choose $b_0=1$, $b_m=0$ $(m\geqq 1)$, $a_\nu=\overline{\alpha(\nu)}\lambda$ $(\nu\leqq n)$, $a_\nu=0$ for $\nu>n$ where λ is chosen to give $\|a\|=1$. Then

$$B^2 = \lambda^2\left(\sum_0^n |\alpha(\nu)|^2\right)^2$$

$$= \sum_0^n |\alpha(\nu)|^2 \leqq M^2$$

as claimed. We have shown (Nehari [27])

Theorem 3.3. *For the Hankel form $\alpha(\mu+\nu)_0^\infty$ to be bounded by M it is necessary and sufficient that an analytic function $g(z)$ exist, regular for $|z|<1$, $g(0)=0$, such that*

$$|\overline{[P(z)]}+g(z)| \leqq M \qquad (|z|<1) \tag{3.51}$$

where $P(z)=\sum_{\nu=0}^{\infty} \overline{\alpha(\nu)} z^\nu$. The exact bound of the form is

$$M = \inf_{Q} \sup_{|z|<1} |\overline{P(z)}+g(z)| \tag{3.52}$$

where

$$Q = \{g \mid g \quad \text{regular in} \quad |z|<1,\, g(0)=0\}\,.$$

As a corollary we obtain the following result.

Theorem 3.4. *Let f be analytic in $|z|\leqq 1$ and have positive real part there except for a simple zero at $z=1$. If*

$$\log f(z) = \sum_{\nu=0}^{\infty} \alpha(\nu) z^\nu \qquad (\alpha(0)=1)$$

then the Hankel matrix $\alpha(\mu+\nu)]_0^\infty$ has exact bound π.

Proof. One candidate for $g(z)$ in (3.52) is

$$g(z) = -\log f(z).$$

This yields the bound

$$\begin{aligned} M &\leqq \sup_{|z|<1} |\log \overline{f(z)} - \log f(z)| \\ &= 2 \sup_{|z|<1} |\arg f(z)| \\ &= \pi. \end{aligned}$$

On the other hand, suppose for some $g(z)$, regular in $|z|<1, g(0)=0$, we have

$$|\log \overline{f(z)} - g(z)| < \pi - \varepsilon$$

for all $|z|<1$ and some $\varepsilon > 0$. Put $h(z) = f(z)^{-1} e^{g(z)}$. Then

$$|2i \arg f(z) - \log h(z)| < \pi - \varepsilon. \tag{3.53}$$

Hence $\log h(z)$ is bounded in the disc and so

$$0 < \varliminf_{\varrho \to 1^-} |h(\varrho e^{i\theta})| \leqq \varlimsup_{\varrho \to 1^-} |h(\varrho e^{i\theta})| < \infty.$$

Now h has no zeros interior to the disc, hence the change in $\arg h(e^{i\theta})$ around the unit circumference is zero, and so the variation of $2 \arg f(z) - \arg h(z)$ is 2π. However by (3.53),

$$|2 \arg f(z) - \arg h(z)| < \pi - \varepsilon$$

and so its total variation could not exceed $2\pi - 2\varepsilon$, a contradiction. Q.E.D.

The Hilbert matrix $(\mu + \nu)^{-1}]_1^\infty$ is the case $f(z) = 1 - z$ of Theorem 3.4.

In Widom [48] Theorem 3.3 is generalized as follows. By the *numerical range* of an operator H on a Hilbert space is understood the image of the unit sphere under the mapping

$$x \to (x, Hx)$$

of the sphere into the complex numbers. The numerical range is always a convex set. Widom determines explicitly the smallest symmetric convex set containing the numerical range of H of a bounded Hankel matrix H.

3.6 Spectral Density

In Eq. (2.77) we gave an asymptotic formula for the number of eigenvalues of the finite sections of the Hilbert integral kernel $(x+y)^{-1}$ which lie in $(\theta\pi, \pi)$. In this section we show that the formula holds for the Hilbert *matrix* also, more precisely, it holds for a large family of

Hankel matrices which contains the Hilbert matrix. The method is closely related to the classical methods which proved the density theorem (2.73) for Toeplitz matrices, namely

(A) If H_N is the Nth finite section of the matrix, by examining the trace of H_N^n determine the growth of $\sum_{i=1}^{N} \lambda_{i,N}^n$.

(B) By taking linear combinations, find the growth of $\sum_{i=1}^{N} P(\lambda_{i,N})$ where P is a polynomial.

(C) Approximate the characteristic function of an interval by polynomials, use the result of (B), and thereby obtain the growth of the number of eigenvalues in that interval.

This program was carried out by Widom [48], under various assumptions on the rate of growth of the sequence $C_\mu]_0^\infty$ which generates the Hankel matrix $C_{\mu+\nu}]_0^\infty$. For our purposes the most useful of these is the assumption

$$C_m \sim L(m)/(m+1) \qquad (m \to \infty) \tag{3.54}$$

where $L(x)$ is absolutely continuous for $x > 0$ and is *slowly varying* in the sense that

$$L'(x)/xL(x) = 0 \qquad (x \geqq x_0). \tag{3.55}$$

Under these hypotheses he proved

Theorem 3.5. *Let a be fixed, $0 < a < 1$. The number of eigenvalues of the matrix*

$$H_N = C_{\mu+\nu}]_{\mu,\nu=0}^N \tag{3.56}$$

which exceed $\pi a L(N)$ is asymptotic to the area in the first quadrant bounded by the curves

$$\begin{aligned} &\text{(a)}\ x = \log N, \\ &\text{(b)}\ L(e^x)\operatorname{sech}\frac{\pi}{2}y = aL(N). \end{aligned} \tag{3.57}$$

The proof is quite technical and we merely outline it here. We have from Trace H_N^n,

$$\begin{aligned} \sum_{j=0}^{N-1} \lambda_{N,j}^n &= \sum_{j_1,\ldots,j_n=0}^{N-1} \frac{L(j_n+j_1)L(j_1+j_2)\ldots L(j_{n-1}+j_n)}{(j_n+j_1+1)(j_1+j_2+1)\ldots(j_{n-1}+j_n+1)} \\ &= \int_0^N \cdots \int_0^N \frac{L(x_n+x_1)\ldots L(x_{n-1}+x_n)}{(x_n+x_1+1)\ldots(x_{n-1}+x_n+1)}\, dx_1 \ldots dx_n + O(L(N)^n). \end{aligned}$$

The integral is estimated, and shown to be between

$$[(1-\varepsilon)I_n + 2\varepsilon] \int_1^N (L(x)^n/x)\,dx$$

and

$$[(1+\varepsilon)I_n + 2\varepsilon] \int_1^N (L(x)^n/x)\,dx$$

where

$$I_n = \int_0^\infty \cdots \int_0^\infty \frac{dt_1 \ldots dt_{n-1}}{(1+t_1 \ldots t_{n-1})(t_1+1)\ldots(t_{n-1}+1)}$$

$$= \int_0^\infty (\pi \operatorname{sech}(\pi/2)^n\,dy\,.$$

There follows the estimate

$$\sum_{j=0}^{N-1} \lambda_{N,j}^n = \int_1^N \int_0^\infty (\pi L(x) \operatorname{sech} \pi y/2)^n\,dy\,dx/x$$

$$+ O\left(L(N)^{n-1} \int_1^N (L(x)/x)\,dx\right) \quad (n \geqq 1)\,.$$

For a polynomial $P(x)$, $P(0)=0$,

$$\sum_{j=0}^{N-1} P(\lambda_{N,j}/L(N)) = \int_1^N \int_0^\infty P\left(\frac{\pi L(x)}{L(n)} \operatorname{sech} \frac{\pi}{2} y\right) dy\,dx/x$$

$$+ O((1/L(N)) \int_1^N (L(x)/x)\,dx)\,. \quad (n \geqq 1)$$

If we approximate the characteristic function of $[\pi a, \infty)$ by a polynomial, the double integral on the right is an approximation to the area mentioned in the statement of the theorem.

For the Hilbert matrix, $L(x) \equiv 1$, and we obtain

$$f_n(\theta) \sim (2/\pi)(\operatorname{sech}^{-1}\theta)\ \log n \quad (n \to \infty) \tag{3.58}$$

in agreement with (2.77) for the integral operator.

3.7 Hankel Determinants

The rate of growth of Hankel determinants

$$\Delta_n = \det C_{\mu+\nu}]^n_{\mu,\,\nu=0} \tag{3.59}$$

is closely connected with asymptotic properties of orthogonal polynomials, and has been extensively studied (see [39]). An interesting variation on the classical problem which has recently been considered concerns the maximization of a Hankel determinant with respect to a measure. Precisely, let $w(x)$ be a weight function for $[a, b]$, let $d\alpha(x)$ be a positive measure for $[a, b]$, define

$$C_\mu = \int_a^b t^\mu w(t)\,d\alpha(t) \qquad (\mu = 0, 1, \ldots) \tag{3.60}$$

and Δ_n by (3.59). For fixed $w(t)$, Δ_n depends upon the choice of the measure α. The problem is to determine the maximum of Δ_n over all choices of α. One can get a good feeling for the size of this maximum without any further hypotheses. We have

$$\begin{aligned}
\Delta_n &= \sum_\pi (\operatorname{sgn}\pi) C_{0+i_0} C_{1+i_1} \ldots C_{n+i_n} \\
&= \sum_\pi (\operatorname{sgn}\pi) \left\{\int_a^b t_0^{0+i_0} w(t_0)\,d\alpha(t_0)\right\} \cdots \left\{\int_a^b t_n^{n+i_n} w(t_n)\,d\alpha(t_n)\right\} \\
&= \int_a^b \cdots \int_a^b \{t_0^0 t_1^1 \ldots t_n^n\} w(t_0) \ldots w(t_n) \left(\sum_\pi (\operatorname{sgn}\pi) t_0^{i_0} \ldots t_n^{i_n}\right) d\alpha(t_0) \ldots d\alpha(t_n) \\
&= \int_a^b \cdots \int_a^b \{t_0^0 t_1^1 \ldots t_n^n\} w(t_0) \ldots w(t_n) \prod_{j<i} (t_i - t_j)\,d\alpha(t_0) \ldots d\alpha(t_n)\,.
\end{aligned}$$

Now make a change of variables $t_i \to t'_{\sigma(i)}$ where σ is a permutation. The discriminant is multiplied by $\operatorname{sgn}\sigma$. Do this for each σ, add, and divide by $(n+1)!$, to find

$$\begin{aligned}
\Delta_n &= \frac{1}{(n+1)!} \int_a^b \cdots \int_a^b \prod_{j<i} (t_i - t_j) w(t_0) \ldots w(t_n) \\
&\qquad \cdot \left(\sum_\sigma \operatorname{sgn}(\pi) t^0_{\sigma(0)} t^1_{\sigma(1)} \ldots t^n_{\sigma(n)}\right) d\alpha(t_0) \ldots d\alpha(t_n) \qquad (3.61) \\
&= \frac{1}{(n+1)!} \int_a^b \cdots \int_a^b \prod_{j<i} (t_i - t_j)^2 w(t_0) \ldots w(t_n)\,d\alpha(t_0) \ldots d\alpha(t_n)\,.
\end{aligned}$$

This shows that the sections of Hankel determinants have a simple probabilistic interpretation: let n points be chosen at random from the probability distribution $d\alpha(t)$ on the interval $[a, b]$. Then their mean square discriminant is, aside from a scale factor, just Δ_n. Now let

$$\Gamma_n = \max_{a \leqq t_0 < t_1 < \cdots < t_n \leqq b} \prod_{j<i} (t_1 - t_j)^2 w(t_0) \ldots w(t_n) \tag{3.62}$$

and suppose the maximum is attained at $t_0^*, \ldots, t_n^*$. Take $\alpha(t)$ to be the measure consisting of equal weights $1/(n+1)$ assigned to the mass points $t_0^*, \ldots, t_n^*$. For this $\alpha(t)$, by (3.61) we shall have

$$\Delta_n = (1/(n+1)^{n+1})\Gamma_n \tag{3.63}$$

and for any $\alpha(t)$ at all,

$$\Delta_n \leqq (1/(n+1)!)\Gamma_n \tag{3.64}$$

from (3.61). Hence

$$1 \leqq ([\max_{\alpha} \Delta_n]/\Gamma_n) \cdot (n+1)^{n+1} \leqq e^{n+1}. \tag{3.65}$$

In the case of the "classical" weight functions $w(t)$ (i.e., $w'/w = at + b$) Schoenberg [33] showed that (3.63) is in fact the exact maximum, and further that the maximizing points $t_0^*, \ldots, t_n^*$ are the zeros of a polynomial which satisfies a differential equation of second order and of which the discriminant can be explicitly written down. The proof relies on a variational method used first by Ulin [43] to settle the case $n = 1$.

First it is easy to show, by Helly's theorem or otherwise, that a maximizing distribution, say $F(x)$, exists. Now suppose $x = t$ is a point of increase of F and that $x = u$ is some other point of $[a, b]$. If $F(t^+) - F(t^-) = \varepsilon_1 > 0$, choose ε such that $0 < \varepsilon < \varepsilon_1$. Make a new measure from $F(x)$ by removing mass ε_1 from the point $x = t$ and putting it at $x = u$. The new measure $F^*(x)$ has moments (3.60) C_ν^* satisfying

$$C_\nu^* - C_\nu = (u^\nu w(u) - t^\nu w(t))\varepsilon. \tag{3.66}$$

If, on the other hand, $F(t^+) - F(t^-) = 0$, then for $h > 0$ we have

$$\varepsilon(h) = \int_{t-h}^{t+h} dF(x) > 0.$$

Remove all of the mass $\varepsilon(h)$ from $[t-h, t+h]$ and add it to the mass at u. Then for the new measure $F^*(x)$ and its moments C_ν^* we have

$$C_\nu^* - C_\nu = (u^\nu w(u) - t^\nu w(t))\varepsilon(h) + \int_{t-h}^{t+h} (t^\nu w(t) - x^\nu w(x)) dF(x). \tag{3.67}$$

In either case (3.66) or (3.67) yields

$$C_\nu^* - C_\nu = (u^\nu w(u) - t^\nu w(t))\varepsilon + o(\varepsilon)$$

for a sequence of $\varepsilon \to 0$. For the determinant Δ_n of (3.59) we have

$$\begin{aligned}\Delta_n(F^*) &= \det(C_{\mu+\nu} + u^{\mu+\nu}w(u) - t^{\mu+\nu}w(t))\varepsilon)^n_{\mu,\nu=0} + o(\varepsilon)\\ &= \Delta_n(F) + \det(C_{\mu+\nu} + u^{\mu+\nu}w(u)\varepsilon)^n_{\mu,\nu=0}\\ &\quad - \det(C_{\mu+\nu} + t^{\mu+\nu}w(t)\varepsilon)^n_{\mu,\nu=0} + o(\varepsilon)\,.\end{aligned}$$

Define the polynomial

$$P_{2n}(x) = \det(C_{\mu+\nu} + x^{\mu+\nu})^n_{\mu,\nu=0} - \det(C_{\mu+\nu})^n_{\mu,\nu=0}$$

and put

$$\phi(x) = P_{2n}(x)w(x)\,. \tag{3.68}$$

Then

$$\Delta_n(F^*) - \Delta_n(F) = (\phi(u) - \phi(t))\varepsilon + o(\varepsilon)\,.$$

Since $\Delta_n(F)$ was assumed maximal we have $\phi(u) - \phi(t) \leqq 0$ which is to say that we have shown

Lemma 1. *Let $x = t$ be a point of increase of the maximizing measure $F(x)$. Then*

$$\phi(t) = \max_{x \varepsilon [a,b]} \phi(x)\,.$$

Hence the only possible points of increase of F are among the points at which ϕ assumes its absolute maximum.

Now F must increase at least at $n+1$ points, for otherwise $C_{\mu+\nu})^n_0$ is of rank n and $\Delta_n = 0$. We would like to conclude that F can increase at most at $n+1$ points. This will follow from Lemma 1 if $\phi(t)$ reaches its maximum at most at $n+1$ points. If w is differentiable,

$$\phi'(t) = w(t)\{P'_{2n}(t) + P_{2n}(t)w'(t)/w(t)\}$$

and so it is here that we must make the assumption that w'/w is linear. Take, for instance, $w(t) = e^{-t}$ on $[0, \infty)$. Then ϕ has at most n relative maxima in $(0, \infty)$ together with a possible maximum at the endpoint $x = 0$.

It follows from (3.61) that

$$\Delta_n(F) = (1/(n+1)^{n+1})\Gamma_n$$

where

$$\Gamma_n = \max_{t_i \geqq 0} e^{-(t_0 + \cdots + t_n)} \prod_{\substack{j<i\\ i,j=0}}^{n} (t_i - t_j)^2\,.$$

The maximum of Γ_n evidently has $t_0 = 0$, and by differentiating with respect to t_k we find

$$t_k g''(t_k) + (2 - t_k) g'(t_k) + n g(t_k) = 0$$

where

$$g(t) = \prod_{i=1}^{n} (t - t_i).$$

Hence the polynomial

$$x g''(x) + (2 - x) g'(x)$$

has degree n, and has the same zeros and leading term as

$$-n g(x)$$

and so for all x

$$x g''(x) + (2 - x) g'(x) + n g(x) = 0$$

which is the differential equation satisfied by the Laguerre polynomial $L_n^{(1)}(x)$. The maximizing measure has equal masses $(n+1)^{-1}$ concentrated at the zeros of $L_n^{(1)}(x)$ and at the origin. This leads to

Theorem 3.6. *If* $F(x)$ *has total mass* 1,

$$C_\nu = \int_0^\infty t^\nu e^{-t} dF(t) \qquad (\nu = 0, 1, \ldots)$$

then

$$|\det C_{\mu+\nu}]_{\mu,\nu=0}^{n}| \leqq e^{-n(n+1)} (1^1 2^2 3^3 \ldots n^n)^2 .$$

The bound is sharp.

For $w(x) = 1$ on $[-1, 1]$,

$$|\det C_{\mu+\nu}]_0^n| \leqq 2^{n(n+1)} (1^1 2^2 3^3 \ldots n^n)^4 n^{-n} \prod_1^{2n} \nu^{-\nu}$$

with equality if and only if $F(x)$ has equal masses at $-1, x_1, \ldots, x_{n-1}, 1$ where

$$(1 - x_\nu^2) P_n'(x_\nu) = 0 \qquad (\nu = 1, \ldots, n-1)$$

where $P_n(x)$ is the Legendre polynomial. The explicit evaluations appearing above depend upon the discriminants of the classical orthogonal polynomials which can be found in [39].

CHAPTER IV

Nonlinear Theory

4.1 Introduction. *A Minimax Principle in l^p*

The work of the preceding two chapters has dealt exclusively with finite sections of those classical inequalities which describe the bound of a linear operator on l^2. Yet there remains the tantalizing inequality of Theorem 1.38

$$\text{(a)}\ \sum_{n=1}^{\infty}\left(\sum_{m=1}^{\infty} K(m,n)x_m\right)^p < k^p \sum x_m^p\,, \qquad \text{(b)}\ k=\int_0^{\infty} K(x,1)x^{-1/p}dx \tag{4.1}$$

in which $K(x,y)$ is homogeneous of degree -1 and the constant k is the best possible one. We have found that the case $p=2$ of (4.1) is already essentially equivalent to the theory of sections of Toeplitz forms. We further found that when $p=2$ the constant k of (4.1) (b) is just one superficial manifestation of the deeper fact that the spectral theory of the sections depends upon the function

$$\int_0^{\infty} K(x,1)x^{-s}dx \tag{4.2}$$

for $s=1/2+i\xi$. One may expect that the sections of (4.1) will depend upon (4.2) for $s=1/p+i\xi$, but this has not been proved. Indeed, for $p\neq 2$ one has available none of the vast resources of linear algebra which are available in the self-dual situation, and recourse must be had to the method of hard analysis.

For the general problem of finite sections in l^p

$$\sum_{n=1}^{N}\left(\sum_{m=1}^{N} (K(m,n)x_m)^p \leqq \lambda_N^p \sum_{n=1}^{N} x_n^p\right) \tag{4.3}$$

only a few precise results are known and these are all consequences of a method developed by de Bruijn to deal with Carleman's inequality, which is essentially (4.3) with

$$K(m,n)=\begin{cases}1/n & m\leqq n\\ 0 & m>n\end{cases} \tag{4.4}$$

which is homogeneous of degree -1, and $p=\infty$. We shall discuss this method in detail in the following sections. For the rest of this section we develop a minimax principle for these inequalities which is quite general, and shows promise of wide applicability.

To reason by analogy with l^2, suppose we have given a matrix A which is real and symmetric, and whose entries are all positive (this is somewhat more than is necessary). Suppose further that we wish to estimate the largest eigenvalue λ_N of A, and that for this purpose we have available a good guess $\underline{x}_0$ to the principal eigenvector. Then we get a lower bound from the quadratic form, say,

$$\lambda_N \geqq (\underline{x}_0, A\underline{x}_0)/(\underline{x}_0, \underline{x}_0) \tag{4.5}$$

and an upper bound from the Perron-Frobenius theorem [1]

$$\lambda_N \leqq \max_{1 \leqq i \leqq N} (A x_0)_i/(x_0)_i\,. \tag{4.6}$$

Thus our guess vector $\underline{x}_0$ yields two-sided bounds. Hence if $\underline{x}_0$ is a clever guess, we can get sharp two-sided estimates for λ_N without ever proving anything, but merely by substituting the guess into (4.5), (4.6). The success of the procedure depends upon the minimax principle

$$\lambda_N = \max_{\|x\|=1} (x, Ax) = \min_{x>0} \max_{1 \leqq i \leqq n} (Ax)_i/x_i\,. \tag{4.7}$$

Now consider the number λ_N of (4.3). Evidently

$$\lambda_N = \max_{\|x\|_p=1} \|Kx\|_p$$

and so from any particular vector $x>0$, we get a lower bound for λ_N,

$$\lambda_N \geqq \|Kx\|_p/\|x\|_p\,.$$

What we propose to derive next is the analogue of (4.6) in l^p, which is to say that we shall exhibit λ_N as the solution of a *minimum* problem.

If $x>0$, $p>1$, N fixed, put

$$J(x) = \max_{1 \leqq r \leqq N} \frac{1}{x_r^{p-1}} \sum_{\nu=1}^{N} K(r, \nu) \left(\sum_{\mu=1}^{N} K(\mu, \nu) x_\mu \right)^{p-1}. \tag{4.8}$$

Then we have [55]

Theorem 4.1. *Let the $N \times N$ matrix K have nonnegative entries and suppose that $K^T K$ has strictly positive entries only. Then*

$$\lambda_N^p = \min_{x>0} J(x)\,. \tag{4.9}$$

[1] This also yields a lower bound, but we prefer the quadratic form, for expository reasons.

Lemma 1. *Put*

$$\xi = \inf_{x>0} J(x).$$

Then there is a vector $x^* > 0$ such that $\xi = J(x^*)$.

Proof. Let

$$A = \left\{\min_{r,s} \sum_{\nu=1}^{N} K(r,\nu)^{p-1} K(s,\nu)\right\} / N^{p-1}.$$

Since $K^T K > 0$ we have $A > 0$. Choose a vector $x_0 > 0$, and since the case $N = 1$ is clear, we can suppose $N \geqq 2$. Now

$$\xi = \inf_{\substack{x>0 \\ J(x) \leqq J(x_0)}} J(x).$$

Suppose some x_i, say $x_1 < \varepsilon$. Since $J(cx) = J(x)$, we can assume that $\sum x_i = 1$. Then some x_i is $\geqq N^{-1}$, say $x_2 \geqq N^{-1}$. Hence

$$\begin{aligned} J(x) &\geqq (1/\varepsilon^{p-1} N^{p-1}) \sum_{\nu=1}^{N} K(2,\nu)^{p-1} K(1,\nu) \\ &\geqq A/\varepsilon^{p-1}. \end{aligned}$$

If

$$\varepsilon < \{A/J(x_0)\}^{1/(p-1)}$$

we would have $J(x) > J(x_0)$. Thus

$$\xi = \inf_{x \in \Omega} J(x)$$

where

$$\Omega = \{x \mid x_i \geqq \{A/J(x_0)\}^{1/(p-1)} \quad (\text{all } i); \quad \textstyle\sum x_i = 1\}.$$

Since Ω is compact, and J is continuous on Ω, the proof is complete.

Lemma 2. *Let $x^* > 0$ be a point at which $J(x)$ assumes its minimum value. Then at x^* we have*

$$\sum_{\nu=1}^{N} \left(\sum_{\nu=1}^{N} K(\mu,\nu) x_\mu\right)^{p-1} K(r,\nu) = \lambda x_r^{p-1} \qquad (r = 1, \ldots, N) \tag{4.10}$$

where $\lambda = J(x^*) = \xi$.

Proof. Let ϕ_r denote the left side of (4.10) and let

$$\lambda = \max_{1 \leqq r \leqq N} \phi_r / x_r^{p-1}.$$

We can suppose that at $x = x^*$,

$$\lambda = \phi_1 / x_1^{p-1} = \cdots = \phi_t / x_t^{p-1}$$

and

$$\phi_r / x_r^{p-1} < \lambda \qquad (r \geqq t+1).$$

By direct computation one finds that for $j \neq r$,

$$(\partial/\partial x_j)(\phi_r/x_r^{p-1}) > 0$$

at x^*. In particular, if $t < n$,

$$(\partial/\partial x_n)(\phi_r/x_r^{p-1}) > 0 \qquad (r = 1, \ldots, t).$$

Thus by decreasing x_n^* by a small amount we can reduce all of

$$\phi_r/x_r^{p-1} \qquad (r = 1, \ldots, t),$$

a contradiction.

Lemma 3. *We have*

$$\max_{\|x\|_p = 1} \|Kx\|_p \geqq \min_{x>0} J(x)^{1/p}.$$

Proof. Let x^* be a maximizing point for $\|Kx\|_p$ subject to $\|x\|_p = 1$. Applying Lagrange multipliers we find that at x^*, Eqs. (4.10) hold, where

$$\lambda = \max_{\|x\|_p = 1} \|Kx\|_p^p.$$

The minimum of $J(x)$ is, however, the smallest λ for which (4.10) holds, by Lemma 2.

Lemma 4. *We have*

$$\max_{\|x\|_p = 1} \|Kx\|_p \leqq \min_{x>0} J(x)^{1/p}.$$

Proof. The reader will recognize in this proof an elaboration of Pólya's idea in his proof of Carleman's inequality (Theorem 1.2), namely to introduce suitable weights before applying an appropriate inequality. Let $\gamma_1, \gamma_2, \ldots, \gamma_N$ denote any set of positive numbers. Then

$$\begin{aligned}
\sum_{n=1}^{N}\left(\sum_{m=1}^{N} K(m,n)x_m\right)^p &= \sum_{n=1}^{N}\left(\sum_{m=1}^{N} (K(m,n)/\gamma_m)x_m\gamma_m\right)^p \\
&= \sum_{n=1}^{N}\left(\sum_{m=1}^{N} [K(m,n)^{1/q}/\gamma_m][K(m,n)^{1-1/q}x_m\gamma_m]\right)^p \qquad \left(\frac{1}{p}+\frac{1}{q}=1\right) \\
&\leqq \sum_{n=1}^{N}\left(\sum_{m=1}^{N} K(m,n)^{p-p/q}x_m^p\gamma_m^p\right)\left(\sum_{m=1}^{N} K(m,n)/\gamma_m^q\right)^{p/q} \\
&= \sum_{n=1}^{N}\left(\sum_{m=1}^{N} K(m,n)\gamma_m^p x_m^p\right)\left(\sum_{m=1}^{N} K(m,n)/\gamma_m^q\right)^{p-1} \\
&= \sum_{r=1}^{N} x_r^p\gamma_r^p \sum_{n=1}^{N} K(r,n)\left(\sum_{m=1}^{N} K(m,n)/\gamma_m^q\right)^{p-1} \\
&\leqq \left[\max_{1\leqq r\leqq N} \gamma_r^p \sum_{n=1}^{N} K(r,n)\left(\sum_{m=1}^{N} K(m,n)/\gamma_m^q\right)^{p-1}\right] \sum_{r=1}^{N} x_r^p.
\end{aligned}$$

Putting $y_m = \gamma_m^{-q}$, the quantity in brackets is recognized to be just $J(y)$. Hence for any $y > 0$.

$$\|Kx\|_p^p \leqq J(y)\,\|x\|_p^p\,.$$

Choosing y to minimize $J(y)$ we have the result stated. Lemmas 3 and 4 yield Theorem 4.1.

The result can be stated in several equivalent forms, *viz.*

$$\begin{aligned}
\max \sum_{m,n=1}^{N} K(m,n)x_m y_n \quad & \left(\|x\|_p = \|y\|_q = 1;\ \frac{1}{p} + \frac{1}{q} = 1\right) \\
&= \max \|Kx\|_p \quad (\|x\|_p = 1) \\
&= \max \|Ky\|_q \quad (\|y\|_q = 1) \\
&= \min_{x>0} \max_{1 \leqq r \leqq N} x_r^{-1/q} \left\{ \sum_{\nu=1}^{N} K(r,\nu) \left(\sum_{\mu=1}^{N} K(\mu,\nu) x_\mu \right)^{p-1} \right\}^{1/p}.
\end{aligned}$$

There is of course a continuous analogue of this discrete minimax principle, namely that

$$\min_{f(x)>0} \max_{1 \leqq x \leqq N} f(x)^{-1/q} \left\{ \int_1^N K(x,y) \left(\int_1^N K(t,y) f(t)\,dt \right)^{p-1} dy \right\}^{1/p} \tag{4.11}$$

is the l_p norm of the integral operator K on the interval $[1, N]$.

We illustrate the use of this principle with a proof of (1.16). We need only choose $f(x) = x^{-1/p}$ in (4.11) to discover that a homogeneous kernel of degree -1 is bounded by M where

$$\begin{aligned}
M^p &= x^{1/q} \int_1^N K(x,y) \left\{ \int_1^N K(t,y)\,t^{-1/p}\,dt \right\}^{p-1} dy \\
&= \int_{x/N}^{x} y^{-1/p} K(y,1)\,dy \left\{ \int_{y/x}^{Ny/x} K(\theta,1)\,\theta^{-1/p}\,d\theta \right\}^{p-1} \\
&\leqq \left\{ \int_0^\infty y^{-1/p} K(y,1)\,dy \right\}^p
\end{aligned}$$

which was to be shown.

4.2 Carleman's Inequality

The first inequality in l^p $(p \neq 2)$ whose finite sections were asymptotically estimated was that of Carleman (Theorem 1.2)

$$\sum_{\nu=1}^{\infty} (a_1 a_2 \ldots a_\nu)^{1/\nu} < e \sum_{\nu=1}^{\infty} a_\nu\,. \tag{4.12}$$

This investigation was carried out by de Bruijn [10]. Let λ_n denote the best constant for the truncated inequality

$$\sum_{\nu=1}^{n} (a_1 \dots a_\nu)^{1/\nu} \leqq \lambda_n \sum_{\nu=1}^{n} a_\nu . \tag{4.13}$$

Then by the usual Lagrange multiplier argument, λ_n is the largest positive value of λ for which the equations

$$\begin{aligned} \lambda\nu(a_\nu - a_{\nu+1}) &= (a_1 \dots a_\nu)^{1/\nu} \qquad (\nu = 1, \dots, n) , \\ a_{n+1} &= 0 \end{aligned} \tag{4.14}$$

admit a positive solution $(a_1, \dots, a_n)$. We can change (4.14) into a simple, two-term recurrence formula by setting

$$h_\nu = \log(a_1 \dots a_\nu)^{1/\nu} - \log a_\nu \tag{4.15}$$

which yields in place of (4.14),

$$\begin{aligned} &\text{(a)}\ h_{\nu+1}(\lambda) = h_\nu(\lambda) + \frac{1}{\nu+1}\left\{\log\left(1 - \frac{1}{\lambda\nu}\, e^{h_\nu(\lambda)}\right)^{-\nu} - h_\nu(\lambda)\right\} \\ &\qquad\qquad (\nu = 1, 2, \dots, n-1) , \\ &\text{(b)}\ h_1(\lambda) = 0 , \\ &\text{(c)}\ h_n(\lambda) = \log(n\lambda) . \end{aligned} \tag{4.16}$$

To summarize, then, λ_n is the largest value of λ such that if we start with $h_1(\lambda) = 0.$ and compute $h_2(\lambda), \dots, h_n(\lambda)$ from (4.16) (a), we will find that $h_n(\lambda) = \log n\lambda$. In particular, if we start with some value of λ, and $h_1(\lambda) = 0$, we may find that the recurrence formula (4.16) (a) breaks down after a certain number of steps, in that we attempt to calculate the logarithm of a negative number. We define the *breakdown index* $N(\lambda)$ as the least integer $\nu > 0$ such that $h_\nu(\lambda) \geqq \log(\nu\lambda)$. If no breakdown ever occurs, *i.e.*, if $h_\nu(\lambda) < \log \nu\lambda$ for all ν then we put $N(\lambda) = +\infty$.

We claim first that $N(\lambda) = +\infty$ for $\lambda \geqq e$. We must show that

$$h_\nu(\lambda) < \log \nu\lambda = \log \nu + \log \lambda \qquad (\lambda \geqq e) .$$

It is evidently enough to show that $h_\nu(\lambda) \leqq 1 - 1/\nu$ $(\nu \geqq 1)$. This is readily established by induction, for if it is true for some ν then for that value of ν,

$$e^{1 - h_\nu(\lambda)} > 1 + \frac{1}{\nu}$$

and by (4.16) (a),

$$h_{\nu+1}(\lambda) < h_\nu(\lambda) + \frac{1}{\nu+1}\left\{\log\left(1 - \frac{1}{\lambda\nu} \cdot \frac{e\nu}{\nu+1}\right)^{-\nu} - h_\nu(\lambda)\right\}$$

and since $\lambda \geqq e$,

$$\begin{aligned} h_{\nu+1}(\lambda) &< h_\nu(\lambda)\left(\frac{\nu}{\nu+1}\right) + \frac{1}{\nu+1}\left\{\log\left(1-\frac{1}{\nu+1}\right)^{-\nu}\right\} \\ &< 1 - \frac{2}{\nu+1} + \frac{1}{\nu+1} \\ &= 1 - \frac{1}{\nu+1} \end{aligned}$$

as required.

Lemma 1. *The* $\{\lambda_\nu\}_1^\infty$ *are a strictly increasing sequence,*

$$\lambda_1 < \lambda_2 < \cdots < e,$$

$h_\nu(\lambda)$ *is defined and decreasing for* $\lambda > \lambda_{\nu-1}$ *and satisfies*

$$\begin{cases} h_\nu(\lambda) > \log(\nu\lambda) & (0 \leqq \lambda < \lambda_\nu) \\ h_\nu(\lambda_\nu) = \log(\nu\lambda_\nu) & \\ h_\nu(\lambda) < \log(\nu\lambda_\nu) & (\lambda > \lambda_\nu). \end{cases}$$

Proof. These facts follow readily from the recurrence (4.16)(a). This lemma will permit us to translate asymptotic information about $N(\lambda)$ for $\lambda \to e^-$ into asymptotic information about λ_n for $n \to \infty$.

Lemma 2. *For* λ *fixed,* $0 \leqq \lambda \leqq e$, *the sequence* $h_\nu(\lambda)$ *increases with* ν, *for* $\nu \leqq N(\lambda)$.

Proof. For such ν we have

$$(1/\nu\lambda)e^{h_\nu(\lambda)} < 1$$

whence

$$\begin{aligned} \log 1\bigg/\left[1 - \frac{1}{\lambda\nu}e^{h_\nu(\lambda)}\right]^\nu &> \log\left[1 + \frac{1}{\lambda}e^{h_\nu(\lambda)}\right] \\ &> \log\left(\frac{1}{\lambda}e^{h_\nu(\lambda)}\right) \\ &> h_\nu(\lambda) \end{aligned}$$

and the result follows from (4.16)(a).

Lemma 3. *Let* $N_1(\lambda)$ *denote the breakdown index with respect to the breakdown condition* $h_\nu(\lambda) \geqq 2$ *in place of* $h_\nu(\lambda) \geqq \log(\lambda\nu)$. *Then*

$$\log N(\lambda) - \log N_1(\lambda) = O(1) \quad (\lambda \to e^-).$$

Proof. Let λ be given, $\lambda < e$, and let $h_{N_1}(\lambda) > 2$ with $N_1 < N$. Then, for $N_1(\lambda) \leqq \nu \leqq N(\lambda)$ we have

$$\begin{aligned} h_{\nu+1}(\lambda) - h_\nu(\lambda) &= \frac{1}{\nu+1}\left\{\log\left(1 - \frac{1}{\nu\lambda} e^{h_\nu(\lambda)}\right)^{-\nu} - h_\nu(\lambda)\right\} \\ &> \frac{1}{\nu+1}\left\{\frac{1}{\lambda} e^{h_\nu(\lambda)} - h_\nu(\lambda)\right\} \\ &\geqq \frac{1}{\nu+1}\{(e^{h_\nu - 1} - h_\nu)/h_\nu^2\} h_\nu^2 \end{aligned}$$

and since $x^{-2}(e^{x-1} - x)$ increases for $x \geqq 2$,

$$h_{\nu+1}(\lambda) - h_\nu(\lambda) \geqq \frac{1}{6(\nu+1)} h^2(\lambda).$$

Hence $h_\nu \geqq k_\nu$ $(\nu = N_1(\lambda), N_1(\lambda)+1, \ldots, N(\lambda))$, where k_ν is defined by $k_{N_1} = h_{N_1}$ and

$$k_{\nu+1} = k_\nu + \frac{1}{6(\nu+1)} k_\nu^2 \qquad (N_1 \leqq \nu \leqq N(\lambda)).$$

Since $h_\nu \leqq \log \lambda\nu$ for these ν, and $\log\lambda\nu \leqq \nu$, we have $k_\nu \leqq \nu$. Thus

$$\begin{aligned} 1/k_\nu - 1/k_{\nu+1} &= 1/k_\nu - 1\bigg/\left\{k_\nu\left[1 + \frac{k_\nu}{6(\nu+1)}\right]\right\} \\ &= 1/(6(\nu+1) + k_\nu) \\ &\geqq 1/(7\nu + 6) \\ &\geqq 1/[7(\nu+1)]. \end{aligned}$$

Summing over ν,

$$1/2 \geqq 1/h_{N_1} > 1/k_{N_1} - 1/k_N > 1/7 \sum_{N_1 \leqq \nu < N} 1/(\nu+1)$$

from which

$$\log N - \log N_1 = O(1)$$

as claimed.

Lemma 4. *For given $p > 0$, there exist $\mu > p$, and β such that $1 < \beta < e$ and*

$$1/2 < h_\mu(\lambda) < \log\lambda - 1/\mu.$$

Proof. We know that

$$h_\nu(e) < 1 - 1/\nu \qquad (\nu \geqq 2).$$

Further, not all of the numbers $h_\nu(e)$ are $\leqq 1/2$, for if so, then recurrence (4.16) (a) would imply

$$\begin{aligned} h_{\nu+1}(e)-h_\nu(e) &> \frac{1}{\nu+1}\{\log(1-1/\nu e^{1/2})^{-\nu}-1/2\} \\ &\geqq \frac{1}{\nu+1}\{e^{-1/2}-1/2\}\,. \end{aligned}$$

But $\sum \frac{1}{\nu+1}$ diverges, so the above cannot hold for all $\nu \geqq 1$. Hence for some integer $\mu > p$ we have

$$1/2 < h_\mu(e) < 1 - 1/\mu$$

and the conclusion follows by continuity.

Lemma 5. *There exist* β, c *such that* (a) $1<\beta<e, c>0$ (b) *for all* λ, $\beta<\lambda\leqq e$ *and all* ν, $1\leqq\nu\leqq N(\lambda)$ we have

$$\frac{1}{\lambda}e^{h_\nu(\lambda)} - h_\nu(\lambda) > c/\sqrt{\nu}\,. \tag{4.17}$$

Proof. By Lemma 4 with $p=2$ we have a $\mu\geqq 3$ and a β such that

$$1/2 < h_\mu(\lambda) < \log\lambda - 1/\mu\,.$$

For all ν such that $h_\nu(\lambda)<\log\lambda$ we claim that

$$h_{\nu+1}(\lambda)-h_\nu(\lambda) < \frac{1}{\nu+1}\left\{\frac{1}{2}(\log\lambda - h_\nu)^2 + \log\left(\frac{e}{\lambda}\right) + \frac{3}{4\nu}\right\}. \tag{4.18}$$

Indeed, from (4.16) (a),

$$\begin{aligned} h_{\nu+1}(\lambda)-h_\nu(\lambda) &= \frac{1}{\nu+1}\left\{\log\left(1-\frac{1}{\lambda\nu}e^{h_\nu(\lambda)}\right)^{-\nu} - h_\nu(\lambda)\right\} \\ &= \frac{1}{\nu+1}\left\{\frac{1}{\lambda}e^{h_\nu(\lambda)} - h_\nu(\lambda) + \frac{e^{2h_\nu(\lambda)}}{2\lambda^2\nu} + \frac{e^{3h_\nu(\lambda)}}{3\lambda^3\nu^2} + \cdots\right\}. \end{aligned} \tag{4.19}$$

Now

$$e^{h_\nu(\lambda)}/\lambda = e^{-u} < 1 - u + u^2/2$$

where $u=\log\lambda - h_\nu(\lambda)$ and since $u>0$, $e^{-u}<1$ and so

$$\frac{1}{2}e^{-u}\nu^{-1} + \frac{1}{3}e^{-2u}\frac{1}{\nu^2} + \frac{1}{4}e^{-3u}\frac{1}{\nu^3} + \cdots < \frac{1}{2\nu} + \frac{1}{3\nu^2} + \frac{1}{4\nu^3} + \cdots < \frac{3}{4}$$

say, since $\nu\geqq\mu\geqq 3$. Substituting in (4.19), we find (4.18), as claimed.

Now for the set of v which we are now considering we have $1/2 < h_\mu \leqq h_v < \log\lambda$ and so from (4.18) there follows

$$h_{v+1} - h_v < \frac{1}{v+1}\left\{\frac{1}{4}(\log\lambda - h_v) + \log\frac{e}{\lambda} + \frac{3}{4v}\right\}, \tag{4.20}$$

which is linear in h_v. If we write

$$t_v = \log\lambda - h_v + 4\log(e/\lambda) - 1/v$$

then (4.20) is simply

$$t_{v+1} > t_v\{1 - 1/4(v+1)\}\,. \tag{4.21}$$

Since $t_\mu > 0$ we have $t_v > 0$ for all of our v. More precisely, since $1 - x/4 > (1-x)^{1/4}$ we have from (4.21)

$$t_{v+1} > t_v \cdot \left(\frac{v}{v+1}\right)^{1/4}$$

and so

$$t_{v+1} \geqq \frac{1}{(v+1)^{1/4}}\,\mu^{1/4} t_\mu \tag{4.22}$$

by induction, for all v such that $h_v < \log\lambda$. We surely have $h_v(\lambda) < \log\lambda$ if $t_v > 4\log e/\lambda$, by definition of t_v. If

$$(\mu/v)^{1/4} t_\mu > 4\log(e/\lambda)$$

then by (4.22), t_v is $> 4\log e/\lambda$. Hence

$$t_v \geqq (\mu/v)^{1/4} t_\mu \tag{4.23}$$

for all v in the range

$$\mu \leqq v < \mu t^4/(4\log e/\lambda)^4 \tag{4.24}$$

and no breakdown can occur here.

To prove the Lemma, the relation $e^{-u} > 1 - u + \frac{1}{3}u^2$ valid for $0 < u < 1$, implies, with $u = \log\lambda - h_v(\lambda)$, that

$$\begin{aligned} e^{h_v(\lambda) - \log\lambda} - h_v(\lambda) &> \log e/\lambda + \frac{1}{3}(\log\lambda - h_v(\lambda))^2 \\ &> (\log e/\lambda)^2 + \frac{1}{3}(\log\lambda - h_v(\lambda))^2 \\ &> \frac{1}{32}(4\log e/\lambda + \log\lambda - h_v(\lambda))^2 \end{aligned} \tag{4.25}$$

where we have used the fact that

$$u^2 + \frac{1}{3}v^2 > u^2 + \left(\frac{1}{4}v\right)^2 > \frac{1}{2}\left(u + \frac{v}{4}\right)^2.$$

Now from (4.23),

$$t_\nu = \log\lambda - h_\nu(\lambda) + 4\log(e/\lambda) > (\mu/\nu)^{1/4} t_\mu$$

and (4.25) implies that the left side of (4.17) is $\geqq \left[\frac{1}{32}(\mu)^{1/2} t_\mu^2\right] 1/\sqrt{\nu}$ in the range (4.24), which proves (5.2) in this range. The remaining values of ν are easily disposed of, and we omit the argument.

Lemma 6. *There is a β such that for each λ in (β, e) we can find an $N < N(\lambda)$ such that $h_N(\lambda) > 2$.*

Proof. Take $p = 2e^3$ in Lemma 4. Then there is a $\mu > 2e^3$ and β $(1 < \beta < e)$ such that

$$1/2 < h_\mu(\lambda) < \log\lambda - 1/\mu.$$

Fixing μ, we have for any $\nu \geqq \mu$ such that $h_\nu(\lambda) < 3$

$$\frac{1}{\nu\lambda} e^{h_\nu(\lambda)} < \frac{1}{2e^3\lambda} e^3 = 1/2\lambda < 1/2.$$

Then from the recurrence (4.16),

$$\begin{aligned} h_{\nu+1}(\lambda) - h_\nu(\lambda) &= \frac{1}{\nu+1}\left\{\log\left(1 - \frac{1}{\lambda\nu} e^{h_\nu(\lambda)}\right)^{-\nu} - h_\nu(\lambda)\right\} \\ &= \frac{1}{\nu+1}\left\{\frac{1}{\lambda} e^{h_\nu(\lambda)} - h_\nu(\lambda) + e^{2h_\nu(\lambda)}\frac{1}{2\lambda^2\nu} + \frac{e^{3h_\nu(\lambda)}}{3\lambda^3\nu^2} + \cdots\right\} \\ &\geqq \frac{1}{\nu+1}\left\{\frac{1}{\lambda} e^{h_\nu(\lambda)} - h_\nu(\lambda)\right\} \\ &\geqq \frac{1}{\nu+1}\log\left(\frac{e}{\lambda}\right). \end{aligned}$$

This relation cannot hold for all $\nu \geqq \mu$ for $\sum(h_{\nu+1} - h_\nu)$ would then diverge. Hence let $h_\sigma(\lambda)$ be < 2 with $h_{\sigma+1}(\lambda) > 2$. It is easy to show that $h_{\nu+1} - h_\nu < 1$ always, so $h_{\sigma+1} < 3$. We can choose $N = \sigma + 1$ to satisfy the requirements of the lemma.

Now, by Lemma 3, we are interested in the number of steps of the recurrence relation which can be carried out without getting $h_\nu(\lambda)$

above 2. Then the right side of this recurrence is of the form

$$\frac{1}{v+1}\left\{\frac{1}{\lambda}e^{h_v(\lambda)}-h_v(\lambda)+e^{2h_v(\lambda)}/2\lambda^2 v+\cdots\right\}.$$

The terms inside the curly brace after the first two are $O(v^{-1})$, while by Lemma 5, the first two terms are $>cv^{-1/2}$. Consequently we neglect all terms but the first two, getting the new recurrence

$$h_{v+1}(\lambda)-h_v(\lambda)=\frac{1}{v+1}\left(\frac{1}{\lambda}e^{h_v(\lambda)}-h_v(\lambda)\right).$$

To estimate the number of steps required to get $h_v(\lambda)>2$ we replace this by the continuous version

$$\frac{d}{dh}[\log(v+1)]=1\bigg/\left(\frac{1}{\lambda}e^h-h\right).$$

Hence the number of steps N satisfies

$$\begin{aligned}\log N &\sim \int_0^2 dh\bigg/\left(\frac{1}{\lambda}e^h-h\right) \qquad (\lambda\to e^-) \qquad (4.26)\\ &=\theta(2)\end{aligned}$$

where

$$\theta(y)=\int_0^y dx\bigg/\left(\frac{1}{\lambda}e^x-x\right).$$

It is straightforward to estimate the errors introduced in these two replacements and thereby to show that (4.26) is actually true. Further, for $\lambda\leqq e$,

$$\begin{aligned}\theta(\infty)-\theta(2) &= \int_0^\infty dx\bigg/\left(\frac{1}{\lambda}e^x-x\right)\\ &\leqq \int_2^\infty dx/(e^{x-1}-x)\\ &= O(1) \qquad (\lambda\to e^-)\end{aligned}$$

and so

$$\log N=\int_0^\infty dx\bigg/\left(\frac{1}{\lambda}e^x-x\right)+O(1) \qquad (\lambda\to e^-)$$

and putting $x=\log\lambda+y$,

$$\log N=\int_{-\log\lambda}^{\infty} dy/(e^y-y-\log\lambda)+O(1) \qquad (\lambda\to e^-),$$

in which the maximum of the integrand is at the origin. Since $\lambda \to e^-$, $\log \lambda$ is near 1, and

$$\log N = \int_{-\infty}^{\infty} \frac{dy}{\left(1+y+\frac{y^2}{2}+\cdots\right)-y-\log\lambda} + O(1)$$

$$= \int_{-\infty}^{\infty} \frac{1}{\frac{y^2}{2}+(1-\log\lambda)} + O(1)$$

$$= \pi\sqrt{2/\log(e/\lambda)} + O(1) \qquad (\lambda \to e^-).$$

Now we can solve the original problem of determining the behavior of λ_n as $n \to \infty$. For, if $\lambda = \lambda_n$ we have $N(\lambda) = n$. Hence

$$\log n = \pi\sqrt{2/\log(e/\lambda_n)} + O(1) \qquad (n \to \infty)$$

which is to say that

$$\lambda_n = e - \frac{2\pi^2 e}{(\log n)^2} + O(1/(\log n)^3) \qquad (n \to \infty) \tag{4.27}$$

completing the study of sections of Carleman's inequality.

The method is notable in that it is a distinctively nonlinear approach, and in that it can be generalized to other inequalities in l^p. This was done by Ackermans [1]. He found, by a direct generalization of the above arguments that the best constants for the following inequalities have the forms shown below. Many others can be handled by the same methods.

(a) *Hardy's Inequality*

$$\sum_{n=1}^{N} \left\{\frac{1}{n}(a_1^p + a_2^p + \cdots + a_n^p)\right\}^{1/p} \leqq \lambda_N(p) \sum_{n=1}^{N} a_n \qquad (0<p<1)$$

$$\lambda_N(p) = (1-p)^{-1/p} - (1-p)^{-1-1/p} 2\pi^2 (\log N)^{-2} + O((\log N)^{-3}),$$

(b) *Inequalities of Copson*

$$(1)\quad \begin{cases} \sum_{n=1}^{N} (a_n + a_{n+1} + \cdots + a_N)^p \leqq \lambda_N(p) \sum_{n=1}^{N} n^p a_n^p \qquad (p>1) \\ \lambda_N(p) = p^p - (p-1)p^{p+1} 2\pi^2 (\log N)^{-2} + O((\log N)^{-3}) \end{cases}$$

$$(2)\quad \begin{cases} \sum_{n=1}^{N} n^{-s}(a_1 + \cdots + a_n)^p \leqq \lambda_N(p, s) \sum_{n=1}^{N} n^{-s}(na_n)^p \qquad (p \geqq s > 1) \\ \lambda_N(p, s) = \left(\frac{p}{s-1}\right)^p - \frac{(p-1)}{(s-1)} \left(\frac{p}{s-1}\right)^{p+1} \frac{2\pi^2}{(\log N)^2} + O((\log N)^{-3}), \end{cases}$$

(c) *Knopp's Inequality*

$$\sum_{n=1}^{N} \left\{\frac{1}{n}(a_1^{-p} + \cdots + a_n^{-p})\right\}^{-1/p} \leqq \lambda_N(p) \sum_{n=1}^{N} a_n \qquad (p > 0)$$

$$\lambda_N(p) = (1+p)^{1/p} - (1+p)^{-1+1/p} 2\pi^2 (\log N)^{-2} + O((\log N)^{-3}).$$

References

1. Ackermans, S. T. M.: An Asymptotic Method in the Theory of Series (Thesis). 83 pp. Eindhofen 1964.
2. Baxter, G.: A convergence equivalence related to polynomials on the unit circle. Trans. Am. Math. Soc. **99**, 471—487 (1961).
3. — A norm inequality for a "finite-section" Weiner-Hopf equation. Illinois J. Math. **7**, 97—103 (1963).
4. — Polynomials defined by a difference system, J. Math. Anal. Appl. **2**, 223—263 (1961).
5. Baxter, G., Hirschman, I. I., Jr.: An explicit inversion formula for finite-section Weiner-Hopf operators. Bull. Am. Math. Soc. **70**, 820—823 (1964).
6. Carleman, T.: Sur les fonctions quasi-analytiques, Conférences faites au cinquième congrès des mathématiciens scandinaves, Helsinki (1932), pp. 181—196.
7. Copsey, E. H., Frazer, H., Sawyer, W. W.: Empirical data on Hilbert's Inequality. Nature **161**, 361 (1948).
8. Davis, J., Hirschman, I. I., Jr.: Toeplitz forms and Ultraspherical Polynomials. Pacific J. Math. **18**, 73—95 (1966).
9. de Bruijn, N. G.: Asymptotic methods in analysis. New York: Interscience 1958.
10. — Carleman's inequality for finite series. Koninkl. Ned. Akad. Wetenschap. Proc. Ser. A **66**, 505—514 (1963).
11. de Bruijn, N. G., Wilf, H. S.: On Hilbert's inequality in *n* dimensions. Bull. Am. Math. Soc. **1962**, 70—73.
12. Fairthorne, R. A., Miller, J. C. P.: Hilbert's double series theorem and principal latent roots of the resulting matrix. Math. Comp. **3**, 399—400 (1949).
13. Frazer, H.: Note on Hilbert's inequality. J. London Math. Soc. **21**, 7—9 (1946).
14. Geronimus, Ya. L.: On certain asymptotic properties of polynomials. Math. Sbornik **65**, 77—88 (1948).
15. — Polynomials Orthogonal on a Circle and Interval. London-New York: Pergamon Press 1960.
16. Grenander, U., Szegö, G.: Toeplitz forms and their applications. Berkeley: 1958.
17. Hardy, Littlewood, Pólya: Inequalities. Cambridge: University Press 1959.
18. Hirschman, I. I., Jr.: Extreme eigenvalues of Toeplitz forms associated with Jacobi polynomials. Pacific J. Math. **14**, 107—161 (1964).
19. — Extreme eigenvalues of Toeplitz forms associated with orthogonal polynomials. J. Anal. Math. **12**, 187—242 (1964).
20. — Finite sections of Weiner-Hopf equations and Szegö polynomials. J. Math. Anal. Appl. **11**, 290—320 (1965).
21. — Finite sections of Weiner-Hopf equations on a compact group with ordered dual. Bull. Am. Math. Soc. **70**, 508—510 (1964).
22. — On a theorem of Szegö, Kac and Baxter. J. Anal. Math. **14**, 225—234 (1965).

23. — Szegö functions on a locally compact Abelian group with ordered dual. Trans. Am. Math. Soc. **121**, 133—159 (1966).
24. — The strong Szegö limit theorem for Toeplitz determinants. Am. J. Math. **88**, 577—614 (1966). See also [5], [8].
25. Kac, M.: Toeplitz matrices, translation kernels and a related problem in probability theory. Duke Math. J. **21**, 501—509 (1964).
26. —, Murdock, W. L., Szegö, G.: On the eigenvalues of certain Hermitian forms. J. Rat. Mech. Anal. **2**, 767—800 (1953).
27. Nehari, Z.: On bounded bilinear forms. Ann. Math. **65**, 153—162 (1957).
28. Parter, S. V.: Extreme eigenvalues of Toeplitz forms and applications to elliptic difference equations, Trans. Am. Math. Soc. **99**, 153—193 (1961).
29. On the extreme eigenvalues of Toeplitz matrices Trans. Am. Math. Soc. **100**, 263—276 (1961).
30. — On the extreme eigenvalues of truncated Toeplitz matrices. Bull. Am. Math. Soc. **67**, 191—196 (1961).
31. Pólya, G.: Proof of an inequality. Proc. London Math. Soc. **24**, (1926), Records of Proceedings, lvii.
32. —, Szegö, G.: Aufgaben und Lehrsätze aus der Analysis. Berlin-Heidelberg-New York: Springer 1964.
33. Schoenberg, I. J.: On the maxima of certain Hankel determinants and the zeros of the classical orthogonal polynomials. Koninkl. Ned. Akad. Wetenschap. Proc. Ser. A (62) **1959**, 282—290.
34. Schur, I.: Bemerkungen zur Theorie der Beschränkten Bilinearformen mit unendlich vielen Veränderlichen, J. Math. **140**, 1—28 (1911).
35. — Über Potenzreihen, die im Innern des Einheitskreises beschränkt sind. J. Reine Angew. Math. **147**, 205—232 (1917).
36. Shohat, J. A., Tamarkin, J. D.: The problem of moments. Am. Math. Soc. Math. Surveys, No. 1, New York 1943.
37. Szegö, G.: A Toeplitz féle formákról, Mathematikai és természettudományi ertesetö 35 (1917), pp. 185—222.
38. — Ein Grenzwertsatz über die Toeplitzschen Determinanten einer reellen positiven Funktion. Math. Ann. **76**, 490—503 (1915).
39. — Orthogonal polynomials. Am. Math. Soc. Colloq. Series, XXIII, 1959. See also [16], [26].
40. Taussky, O.: A remark concerning the characteristic roots of the finite segments of the Hilbert matrix. Quart. J. Math. Oxford, Ser. **2**, 80—83 (1964).
41. Titchmarsh, E. C.: Introduction to the theory of Fourier integrals. Oxford: 1948.
42. Todd, J.: The condition of the finite segments of the Hilbert matrix, Contributions to the solution of systems of linear equations and the determination of eigenvalues, Nat. Bur. Std. Applied Math. Ser. No. 39, U.S. Govt. Printing Office, Washington, D.C., 1954, pp. 109—116.
43. Ulin, B.: On a conjecture of Nelder in mathematical statistics. Comp. Math. **13**, 148—149 (1957).
44. Wang, Ju-Kwei: Note on a theorem of Nehari on Hankel forms, to appear.
45. Widom, H.: Extremal polynomials associated with a system of curves in the complex plane, Advances in Mathematics, Vol. 3 (2), April 1969, pp. 127—232.
46. — Extreme eigenvalues of N-dimensional convolution operators. Trans Am. Math. Soc. **106**, 391—414 (1963).
47. — Extreme eigenvalues of translation kernels. Trans. Am. Math. Soc. **100**, 252—262 (1961).
48. — Hankel matrices. Trans. Am. Math. Soc. **121**, 1—35 (1966).

49. — On the eigenvalues of certain Hermitian operators. Trans. Am. Math. Soc. **88**, 491—522 (1958).
50. — Polynomials associated with measures in the complex plane. J. Math. Mech. **16**, 997—1014 (1967).
51. — Stable processes and integral equations, Trans. Am. Math. Soc. **98**, 430—449 (1961).
52. Widom, H., Wilf, H. S.: Small eigenvalues of large Hankel matrices. Proc. Am. Math. Soc. **17**, 338—344 (1966).
53. Wilf, H. S.: Dirichlet series and Toeplitz forms. J. Math. Anal. Appl. **1964**, 45—51.
54. — Finite sections of the classical inequalities. Koninkl. Ned. Akad. Wetenschap. Proc. Ser. A **24**, 340—342 (1962).
55. — A minimax principle of Perron-Frobenius type for operator norms in l^p, to appear. See also [11], [52].

Subject Index

Typesetting, Printing and Binding: Brühlsche Universitätsdruckerei Gießen

Ergebnisse der Mathematik und ihrer Grenzgebiete

1. Bachmann: Transfinite Zahlen. DM 38,–; US $ 10.50
2. Miranda: Partial Differential Equations of Elliptic Type. DM 58,–; US $ 16.00
4. Samuel: Méthodes L'Algèbre Abstraite en Géométrie Algébrique. DM 26,–; US $ 7.20
5. Dieudonné: La Géométrie des Groupes Classiques. DM 38,–; US $ 10.50
6. Roth: Algebraic Threefolds with Special Regard to Problems of Rationality. DM 19,80; US $ 5.50
7. Ostmann: Additive Zahlentheorie. 1. Teil: Allgemeine Untersuchungen. DM 38,–; US $ 10.50
8. Wittich: Neuere Untersuchungen über eindeutige analytische Funktionen. DM 28,–; US $ 7.70
11. Ostmann: Additive Zahlentheorie. 2. Teil: Spezielle Zahlenmengen. DM 28,–; US $ 7.70
14. Coxeter/Moser: Generators and Relations for Discrete Groups. DM 32,–; US $ 8.80
16. Cesari: Asymptotic Behavior and Stability Problems in Ordinary Differential Equations. DM 36,–; US $ 9.90
17. Severi: Il teorema di Riemann-Roch per curve, superficie e varietà questioni collegate. DM 23,60; US $ 6.50
18. Jenkins: Univalent Functions and Conformal Mapping. DM 34,–; US $ 9.40
19. Boas/Buck: Polynomial Expansions of Analytic Functions. DM 16,–; US $ 4.40
20. Bruck: A Survey of Binary Systems. DM 36,–; US $ 9.90
21. Day: Normed Linear Spaces. DM 17,80; US $ 4.90
25. Sikorski: Boolean Algebras. DM 38,–; US $ 9.50
26. Künzi: Quasikonforme Abbildungen. DM 39,–; US $ 10.80
27. Schatten: Norm Ideals of Completely Continous Operators. DM 26,–; US $ 7.20
28. Noshiro: Cluster Sets. DM 36,–; US $ 9.90
29. Jacobs: Neuere Methoden und Ergebnisse der Ergodentheorie. DM 49,80; US $ 13.70
30. Beckenbach/Bellman: Inequalities. DM 30,–; US $ 8.30
31. Wolfowitz: Coding Theorems of Information Theory. DM 27,–; US $ 7.50
32. Constantinescu/Cornea: Ideale Ränder Riemannscher Flächen. DM 68,–; US $ 18.70
33. Conner/Floyd: Differentiable Periodic Maps. DM 26,–; US $ 7.20
34. Mumford: Geometric Invariant Theory. DM 22,–; US $ 6.10
35. Gabriel/Zisman: Calculus of Fractions and Homotopy Theory. DM 38,–; US $ 9.50
36. Putnam: Commutation Properties of Hilbert Space Operators and Related Topics. DM 28,–; US $ 7.70
37. Neumann: Varieties of Groups. DM 46,–; US $ 12.60
38. Boas: Integrability Theorems for Trigonometric Transforms. DM 18,–; US $ 5.00
39. Sz.-Nagy: Spektraldarstellung linearer Transformationen des Hilbertschen Raumes. DM 18,–; US $ 5.00
40. Seligman: Modular Lie Algebras. DM 39,–; US $ 9.75
41. Deuring: Algebren. DM 24,–; US $ 6.60
42. Schütte: Vollständige Systeme modaler und intuitionistischer Logik. DM 24,–; US $ 6.60
43. Smullyan: First-Order Logic. DM 36,–; US $ 9.90
44. Dembowski: Finite Geometries. DM 68,–; US $ 17.00
45. Linnik: Ergodic Properties of Algebraic Fields. DM 44,–; US $ 12.10
46. Krull: Idealtheorie. DM 28,–; US $ 7.70
47. Nachbin: Topology on Spaces of Holomorphic Mappings. DM 18,–; US $ 5.00
48. Ionescu Tulcea/Ionescu Tulcea: Topics in the Theory of Lifting. DM 36,–; US $ 9.90
49. Hayes/Pauc: Derivation and Martingales. DM 48,–; US $ 13.20
50. Kahane: Series de Fourier Absolument Convergentes. DM 44,–; US $ 12.10
51. Behnke/Thullen: Theorie der Funktionen mehrerer komplexer Veränderlichen. DM 48,–; US $ 13.20
52. Wilf: Finite Sections of Some Classical Inequalities. DM 28,–; US $ 7.70
53. Ramis: Sous-ensembles analytiques d'une variété banachique complexe. En préparation.
54. Busemann: Recent Synthetic Differential Geometry. In preparation.